Ohio Reading Circle
1979   9th

Crazy
To
Fly

Crazy

To

Fly

MARTHA ORR CONN

Illustrated by Richard Cuffari

Atheneum   **1978**   New York

Library of Congress Cataloging in Publication Data
Conn, Martha Orr.
Crazy to Fly.

SUMMARY: In 1918, after his first exposure to flying, a
young farm boy determines to be a pilot despite his father's
bitter opposition.
[1. Air pilots—Fiction. 2. Flying—Fiction] I. Title.
PZ7.C76185Ch   [Fic]   77–23871
ISBN 0-689-30616-4

Published simultaneously in Canada by
McClelland & Stewart, Ltd.
Manufactured in the United States of America by
American Book–Stratford Press
Saddle Brook, New Jersey
Designed by Marjorie Zaum
First Edition

For the three pilots I live with
Bill, Rick, and Dave,
and for the fourth
Rob
who has flown on ahead
and waits to show us
what lies beyond the farthest horizon

Introduction

ALTHOUGH IT IS FICTION, I HAVE TRIED TO MAKE THIS story as historically accurate as possible. In a few places, I have purposely telescoped events—which actually occurred a short time earlier or later—into this year of Tommy's life. Most of these instances concern certain stunts done in the air shows, and I believe it is reasonable to assume that, if they were being recorded a short time later, someone, somewhere, was performing them in 1918 or 1919.

To tell Tommy's story, I needed a great deal of information about those early days and about aviation. I would like to acknowledge the help of the many people who either answered my questions or directed me to someone who could. I cannot name them all, but I do wish to offer special thanks to the following:

Mrs. Clifford Ball

William L. Bekenstein, M.D.
May Ball Hurst
Thomas W. Hurst
Mrs. Phoebe F. Omlie
Mr. and Mrs. Laird E. Orr
Captain Leonard W. Padgett
Mrs. Louise Thaden
James J. Wagner

And to Tom D. Crouch, Assistant Curator, National Air and Space Museum, Smithsonian Institution, who had the patience to read the first completed draft of the manuscript and point out historical inaccuracies.

These people have tried to keep me on course in describing what it was really like back then. If any inaccuracies have crept in, however, I alone am responsible.

I cannot end without a special acknowledgment to a fine writer and a dear friend, Carol Farley. Without her understanding and encouragement, this book would never have been completed.

Marty Conn
Fairfax, Virginia 1977

Crazy
To
Fly

Chapter

1

TOMMY DAVISON HEARD FOOTSTEPS APPROACHING THE barn. He paused in his work and made a face. "Well," he muttered, "if that's Pap, I guess I'm in trouble." But the awkward figure that appeared in the doorway was not his father. It was only Mark.

Tommy's younger brother stopped dead, the two empty milk pails he had been twirling interrupted in midswing. "Holy cow, Tom, what have you done to Pap's new car?" Mark's eyes darted from the gaping hole under the 1916 Model T's laid-back hood to the mess of bolts and other parts strewn around on the floor.

Tommy smiled, but he understood the panic on Mark's freckled face. Mark not only looked like Ma, he worried like her, too. This automobile had been new for over two years, and Pap still treated it as carefully as he had on the day he drove it home from Pittsburgh. The boys weren't even allowed to wash its shiny black sides.

"Don't worry, Mark. It's not half as bad as it looks." Tommy brushed back a lock of reddish-brown hair, adding one more streak of grease to his forehead. "Just don't move anything—I have all these parts in order."

"Are you crazy?" If Pap comes out and sees this . . ." Mark's warning faded as Tommy's head and shoulders disappeared into the space where the scattered parts should have been assembled.

In spite of its muffled sound, Tommy's answer was determined. "I'm hoping Pap won't see it until I get it finished."

"Get what finished? What are you trying to do?"

Tommy pulled back from under the hood and reached for a flat object lying to one side. "Remember that awful noise the car was making when Pap drove it yesterday? I was pretty sure I'd heard that sound before—and I was right!" Proudly he held up the blown gasket. "See the hole in this, Mark? That's why the car was choking and gasping like that. It's an easy thing to fix, though. I helped Mr. Miller put a new gasket on his Model T a couple months back. Lucky thing for us he bought two gaskets while he was at it."

"So that's why you went tearing over to Miller's last night." Mark hesitated, running his fingers nervously through his curly hair. "But are you sure you really know what you're doing? Pap will . . ."

Tommy looked straight across into Mark's eyes. Though his brother was almost two years younger, they were the same height. "Pap will be tickled pink if I can get Black Beauty here running right. Then he won't have to pay John Willis to have a look at it. Now don't get so fussed, Mark. Just go on with your milking. So far as I know, you never saw a thing."

With one last, scared glance over his shoulder, Mark hurried down the steps to the barn's lower level. Tommy turned back to study the parts strewn around the barn floor. "Let's see now," he murmured looking at a large rectangular piece of machinery. "I guess I'm ready to put the head back into place."

Crouching and taking a firm grip, he gave a soft grunt as he rose, then carried the head across and settled it over its new gasket.

"Now comes the tricky part," he muttered. With great care he screwed each bolt down until it began to resist his turning. When all the bolts were in place, he started around again, tightening each one just a little. Mr. Miller had made a point of this—unless all the bolts were tightened evenly, the sealing effect of the new gasket could be ruined.

At last Tommy straightened, glancing over the floor as he wiped his grimy fingers on a rag. Well, no parts left over anyway. He grinned. Mark would be relieved. Lowering the hood back into place, he gave it a final wipe and started toward the pump. After he filled the radiator, he'd better wash up and get on with the milking. No matter how well Beauty ran, Pap wouldn't forgive anyone who neglected chores.

Mark had finished with his cows and was gone by the time Tommy started down the row of milkers assigned to him. A grumble from his stomach reminded Tommy that he had been up much longer than he usually was before he ate. He decided that after breakfast would be soon enough to mention his work to Pap.

When Tommy entered the kitchen, Ma jumped up to bring his plate of pancakes and sausage from its warming place on the stove. "Where in the world have you been, son? Another few minutes and these would have been all dried out," Ma scolded, as she set his plate on the table and then brought the milk pitcher to fill his glass.

"I'm sorry, Ma." Tommy hurried to add butter and syrup to the pancakes. "I got kind of busy this morning." He glanced across to Pap, hoping he'd ask "Busy with what?" but Pap seemed not to hear. He was holding his cup out, signaling for Ma to refill it.

As Tommy chewed on a large bite of sausage, he watched Ma. She was a big woman, but she hurried between the stove and table with brisk efficiency as she filled Pap's coffee cup and then gave Mark the half cup he was allowed now. Once her hair had been the same fiery shade as Mark's, but now her curls were striped with gray. She glanced over at Tommy's fast-emptying plate and warned, "Not so fast, Tommy. You'll choke yourself!" Her round face, flushed pinker than usual from the kitchen's heat, took on an inquiring look as she held her coffeepot toward Tommy's cup.

"No thanks, Ma." Mischievously he quoted her often-voiced objection. "It'll stunt my growth." He swallowed the last bites of pancake and said, "See you outside, Pap." As he pushed back his chair, he was deciding that he'd sit on the side porch until Pap finished and started for the barn. Then he could ask him to try the car. He was careful on the way out to catch the screen door and close it gently behind him, remembering how his father grumbled if anyone let it slam. Settling into the porch swing, Tommy wondered how Pap would act. It was pretty hard to guess about him. Even if the car ran like new, Pap might still have a fit that Tommy had dared to work on it.

Tommy's thoughts were interrupted by a faint noise, which seemed to come from beyond the hills to the east. At first the sound was a little like a Model T engine. But, as the roar grew louder, Tommy became certain that it was not being made by any of the cars or trucks in the neighborhood. He sat up, puzzled. Had a stranger blundered onto the washboard road that joined their farm with the town of Anna's Corner?

Squinting to shut the morning sun out of his eyes, Tommy saw a small speck that incredibly was not on the road, but in the sky above it.

"An airplane!" Tommy gasped. "An honest-to-God airplane!" In his amazement he had echoed one of Pap's favorite expressions, forgetting how Ma felt about it.

Soon Tommy could see the red and silver stripes that fanned out over the two sets of wings. There was some kind of writing on the ship's side. It seemed to be in very large letters, but Tommy couldn't make out what they said. He heard the screen door slam as Mark came running out. "It's an airplane! What the dickens is it doing out here, Tom? You s'pose he's lost?"

Pap was close on Mark's heels, his cup of coffee still clutched in one hand. "If you kids don't quit letting that door slam, I'll . . ."

Pap forgot his threat as he stared at the plane now crossing almost directly overhead. "Well, I'll be a . . ." His words were drowned in a noisy backfire from above. "What's a contraption like that doing in this country?"

From old habit, Pap brushed back a forelock of hair

that was no longer there as he gazed upward. His eyes widened. "He better not be figuring on plopping down in my cow pasture. Them cows are giving little enough now without being scared into going clear dry!"

The plane was almost to the western hills. Pap needn't worry about its landing in his fields. But Tommy was sure that it was much lower now than it had been when he first saw it. As the silvery tail disappeared behind the trees, Pap shrugged and turned away. "You boys get to the rest of your chores."

Tommy didn't move. His ears strained after the receding motor noise. In a moment it seemed to change. It softened and almost died out. Then it roared up again, louder than ever, for several minutes before it quit altogether. "What do you suppose is happening?" he asked Mark. Mark shook his head.

"Get to work now, I'm telling you! This here grass will be up to my knees soon." Tommy jumped at Pap's second, much louder order. Mark scurried over, grabbed the woven straw basket that hung by the kitchen door and hightailed it for the hen house. Tommy threw a resentful glance at his father's back before he stomped across the side lawn and jerked the toolshed door open.

"Get to work! Get to work! That's all we ever hear," he thought. "You'd think he'd want to watch it, too. You'd think he'd at least be a little bit curious." Tommy nudged a shovel and two hoes out of the way, then yanked the push mower from its dusty corner. He paused a moment, his eyes dreamy.

"I wonder where it was going? Boy, I'd give anything to see an airplane close up!" He frowned and kicked the shed door closed. "But we'll never get the chance around here. All we ever get to do are these miserable, everlasting chores!"

Tommy was just finishing his second swath around the large front lawn when he saw his brother pause as he left the hen house and stand staring toward the woods that covered the hill behind their home. Deserting his basket of eggs, Mark began to run toward Tommy. His mouth was moving as he pointed at the trees, but the clank and rattle of the mower drowned his shout. Tommy stopped.

"He's back!" Mark was yelling. "I saw it! He's back!"

"Who? What? *Sh-h-h!*" said Tommy as his ears detected the faint roar. Was it . . . ? It was! The airplane's motor could just barely be heard.

The boys gazed for a long time at the sky above the western hills, but Tommy could see nothing. Finally Mark spoke, disappointment in his voice, "I did see him, Tommy. Just for a minute in that gap there—between the two oak trees. He was flying real low."

"He must be right over the Miller's farm. Listen!" Again Tommy heard the sound, a quiet pause, then a roar before absolute silence. He swung around and grasped Mark's forearm. "Let's go see!"

The delight that appeared on Mark's face faded at once. "But what about Pap, Tommy? He'll skin us if we don't finish our chores first."

Tommy dropped Mark's arm and stepped away. "If we finish first, that airplane will be gone. I've got to see it. You can come or not, just as you please."

He left the mower where it stood and began to run for the path that led upward through the thick woods and over into the hillside pastures of the Miller farm. Mark hesitated for only a moment. Then he ran to catch up.

9

Chapter

2

AT THE PACE TOMMY SET, THE STEEP CLIMB THROUGH the woods took only ten minutes. Both boys were panting when they reached the edge of the wild blackberry patch that crowned the hill. Mark slowed, catching his breath while he chose the best way around the bushes. But Tommy plunged straight on, not feeling the brambles that caught at his faded overalls and bare arms. His attention was fixed on getting to where he could see.

He stopped at the crest of the hill, his knees shaking. He had been so afraid that they would be too late! But the plane was still there.

Beyond the hill pastures, past the matured stalks of corn, the twin wings gleamed at the edge of the Miller's alfalfa field. A small crowd of people stood around, and the boys could see several farm trucks and cars, as well as many horse-drawn vehicles, hurrying up the Miller's lane.

"I guess we aren't the only ones who decided to come and see," Mark gasped. He dropped onto a flat rock where he had a clear view of the excitement below.

Tommy took no time to answer. He ran on down the berry field and leaped the wire fence onto a cow path that would bring him out at the Miller's barn. His eyes scarcely left the biplane. He knew that he had to get closer to it, as close as possible.

The crowd was much larger when Tommy reached its outer edge. A few suits and wide, flowered hats among the dingy overalls and bright aprons of the farm families showed that the townspeople were beginning to arrive. The Miller's dog, tied to a porch railing, was in a frenzy —doing his duty as he saw it by barking at friend and stranger alike.

Tommy cut around the people bunched on the lane side of the field, climbed over the rail fence and went through the freshly mown alfalfa to the far side of the aircraft. How beautiful it was! Crimson red, sparkling silver, and those black letters a foot high on each side. No wonder he hadn't been able to read them—they were printed upside down!

As he bent his head perilously to one side, trying to make the letters out, an amused voice said, "JEFF JOHNSON is what it says. He paints it like that because he claims that when he flies, he's upside down as much as he's right side up. Now stand up before you fall like the other hicks who tried that—and end up combing cow manure out of your hair."

In spite of himself, Tommy glanced downward. He knew that the Miller cows did sometimes graze in this field. Only the sweet-smelling alfalfa stems were crushed

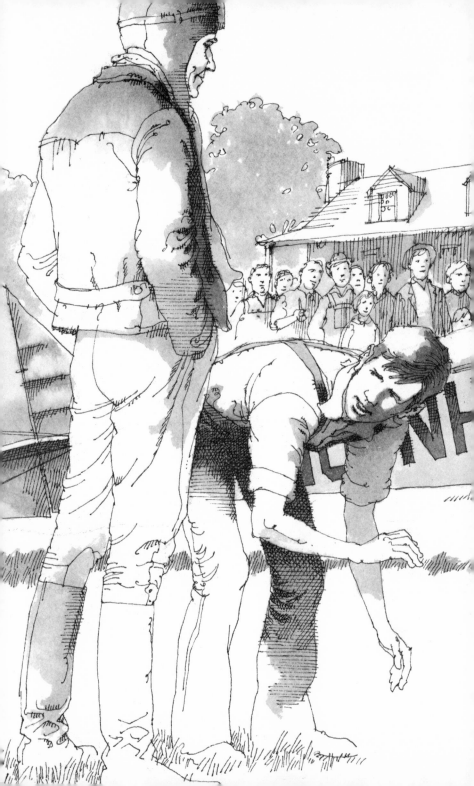

under his worn clodhoppers, but to one side was a tall pair of dull brown leather boots. His eyes followed the leather upward as he straightened. The boots finally ended just below the man's knees. A pair of muddy whipcord jodhpurs came next, then a worn leather jacket, hanging open to display a creased white scarf.

The big man grinned good-naturedly as Tommy's eyes rose further to inspect his tightly fitting leather helmet with its goggles pushed above his forehead. "Outlandish outfit, ain't it?" He scratched a scraggly gray eyebrow. "My partner over there says this is the way folks expect a pilot to dress. But I keep wondering when they're going to bring Jeff a horse to ride. He never looked that pretty when he was flying in the war!"

He gestured to a man—it must be Jeff Johnson himself!—who stood on the far side of the airplane. The other pilot's clothes were the same, but there was a difference. His boots were polished until they gleamed. His tan breeches were spotless. His jacket looked new and was buttoned up to the neck, where his white scarf was tied in an elegant knot. His leather helmet dangled carelessly from one hand, leaving his wavy blond hair free to be admired by the giggling girls around him. To complete the costume, he held a riding crop. This he used to motion toward the airplane.

"Come, lovely ladies. You'll never get a chance like this again. Only a penny a pound for a ride. Don't you want to see what your own house looks like from the air?"

The girls dropped their eyes shyly and backed away, still giggling. From behind them, a huge farmer pushed forward. "Well, I sure do," he bawled, holding up two bills. "It'll cost me two dollars, but it's worth it."

Several people in the crowd snickered. They knew, as Tommy did, that Mr. Lankhorn was closer to two hundred and fifty than to two hundred pounds, but the pilots didn't seem to notice. Jeff, moving with a limp that he tried to conceal, took the weighty passenger's arm and led him toward the machine.

"Yes sir! Right this way, sir. Here's a man knows value when he sees it, George. Give him a hand up." Tommy's companion had moved to the other side of the airplane and was ready to help the fat man wedge himself into the forward seat.

As Jeff rebuttoned the flap of his jacket pocket over the two dollars, his eyes lit on Tommy. "You there, lad. Over here, please," he ordered. Tommy hurried around to stand near George.

"Don't want to run over any prospective customers," Jeff confided to his audience. "Okay, George, he's all yours." Jeff waved his partner toward the rear cockpit.

George winked at Tommy and whispered, "He gets the pretty girls—I get the old men and kids." He shrugged, stepped onto the reinforced wing section next to the fuselage, and hoisted himself into the seat.

"Move back, please, folks. We're about to start her up." Jeff stalked along the railing making shooing motions at those who had been bold enough to cross the fence.

Just as Jeff pulled on the propeller and the engine started up, two small boys slipped back under the rail. Tommy caught them as they reached toward the silvery paint.

"Oh, no you don't. You heard the man." Carrying one

under each arm, Tommy placed them back out of harm's way while the plane taxied down the field.

Jeff nodded. "Good work, young man. Stick around, I can use you. Give you a ride at the end of the day if you'll help out."

A ride! Tommy could hardly believe his luck. He jumped to obey Jeff's orders. Keep the crowd back. Bring a bucket of water. Wipe oil off the fuselage. Polish that windshield. See if Mrs. Miller will trade some sandwiches for a free ride. (She wouldn't ride, but sent Tommy back with a generous lunch.)

Over and over, Tommy lovingly cleaned the airplane, imagining how it would be when it was his turn to sit up there. He would hear George shout, "Clear?" from the seat behind him. Jeff would reply, "Clear!" and ask his own question, "Switch off?" George would check, then nod. "Switch off!" he'd yell. Jeff would pull the propeller around to an easily grasped position. "Contact!" he would shout up to George. George would move the ignition switch to the "On" position and yell back, "Contact!"

With luck, the engine would cough into life the first time Jeff pulled the propeller through its circle. Then they would be off, taxiing down the field. They would turn into the wind and race over the green runway to soar above the barbed wire fence at the end.

Each time the airplane lifted from the field to circle over the neighboring farms and return, Tommy felt that he was riding along. He even experienced strange qualms in his stomach when Jeff went up to—as he put it— "show the crowd how to read my name." The black letters were upright for long, dizzying moments as Jeff performed his breathtaking stunts.

The day rushed on. Tommy could hardly believe it when he saw that the sun was beginning to drop toward the western horizon. A few townsmen were already turning their cars and buggies around, not taking any chances on traveling the rough road home in less than full daylight. Jeff surveyed the waning crowd.

"Okay, folks, this will be the last one," he warned. "Your last chance to see your world as a bird sees it." A plump farm wife edged forward. She blushed with gratitude as Jeff estimated her weight a good twenty pounds low. George gave her a short ride, barely more than around the edges of the farm, but she seemed content as they taxied in.

"Okay, George. Keep that engine running. Got to make Pittsburgh before nightfall." Jeff's brusque tone turned to honey as he waved and yelled to the crowd. "Thanks a lot, folks. It's been a real pleasure meeting you. Lovely country you have here." He turned back and began to climb toward the seat just vacated by the last customer.

"But ... my ride." Tommy shouted over the engine. "You said I could have a ride." George glanced in disgust toward Jeff as the pilot paused on the wing to reply.

"What? Oh ... your ride. Yeah, well, I'm sorry kid. Can't do it today. We're running late. Maybe some other time." Jeff lowered himself into the cockpit and called back over his shoulder, "Always collect your pay before the show, boy. That's rule number one in this business."

There was embarrassment on George's face. "I didn't know he'd promised you, kid. I'm sorry." He began to push the throttle forward while Tommy stood, stunned and unmoving, by the wing. George glanced at him again. "Look, we got to get to Pittsburgh now," he shouted. "Come on down there someday, and I'll make him pay up. My name's George Letic. Ask anyone—they all know me. You hear?"

Tommy nodded and stepped back automatically as the engine roared and the airplane taxied out to begin its run down the field. Once more he watched it lift over the wire fence and turn away toward the south. This time, it did not circle, but sped on into the distance and disappeared.

Tommy turned away and began to trudge toward home. He'd been cheated out of a day's work, he hadn't done his chores, and Pap was going to be furious with him. Yet, strangely, he felt elated. He knew now, as if he'd known it forever, what he wanted to do with his life. Somehow, some way, he and airplanes were meant to be together. He didn't notice when the path steepened. His mind was busy with plans for getting to Pittsburgh.

Chapter

3

"UGH!" TOMMY REACHED UP TO BRUSH AWAY THE
dusty cobweb that had attached itself to his hair when
he straightened. His back ached from bending to shovel
out the chicken coop's far corners. Thank goodness he
was almost finished.

"Lucky Mark!" Tommy thought as he flung his
shoulders far back trying to ease their cramping. Mark
had made it back to the farm and finished his chores
before Pap noticed he was missing. Today he was at the
church picnic with their folks while Tommy, in disgrace,
had been ordered to stay behind and clean the hen house.

"He'd better remember to bring me a piece of Mrs.
Cranby's devil's food cake," Tommy muttered. The
reek of his surroundings faded as Tommy's memory
replaced it with the wonderful aromas that would hover
over the picnic tables. Fried chicken. Glazed hams. Corn

on the cob. Potato salad. Fresh fruit pies. And many-layered cakes.

He sighed. Pap sure had known what punishment would hurt the most. And he hadn't even mentioned the car. Did he think it had fixed itself? Tommy heaved a final shovelful of manure-matted straw into the wheelbarrow outside. Now he only had to cover the floor and fill the nest boxes with fresh straw.

"Not that these stupid birds will use the nests anyway," he grumbled. He was thinking of the many times he'd searched out stray eggs in the muddy corners of the chicken yard. "One thing for sure." Tommy banged the coop door shut, fastened it, and stretched tall. "When I get to running my own life, I am never, *ever* going to raise chickens."

Back in his room, Tommy rubbed a towel across hair still wet from a quick shampoo under the backyard pump. He studied the newspaper clippings that he and Mark had fastened to the white-washed walls of their attic bedroom. It was strange—at the time he'd thought he was just saving the most exciting war news. Now he noticed that every one of his stories involved airplanes. The oldest, a yellowed clipping dated August of 1914, was headlined, OBSERVER PLANES SAVE ENGLISH FORCES FROM ENCIRCLEMENT.

Tommy tried to imagine how these English pilots must have felt. Looking down on the battlefield, they had seen their French allies being driven back on the right side of the British troops. German units had rushed through this break, intent on surprising the English from behind. The men in the plane above must have been sick with fear as they turned to race back to their landing field. What if their warning were not given in time? But it had been, and the English soldiers were able to retreat before they could be cut off and slaughtered.

"How about that, Pap?" Tommy smiled to himself knowing that it was safe to talk back to his father only when he wasn't there. "You s'pose those soldiers think that 'Airplanes are only toys for the rich'?"

Tommy stepped over to his newest clipping. He hadn't paid much attention when Ma first mentioned it.

"Would you look at this Bert?" She'd pointed out a photograph in the newspaper. "Here's that Vernon Castle. Remember when we went to see him and his wife Irene? My, how they could dance!" Tommy's father, deep into the latest farm prices, just grunted. "I sure am glad he wasn't killed when he was shot down. Paper says he's coming back to this country now to teach new pilots. He's an ace—what did you say that meant, Tommy?"

"He's shot down five or more enemy planes," Tommy had answered. Leaning over the back of his mother's rocker, he'd studied the picture, looking not at the pilot, but at his plane. Even in its drab Army colors, it looked a lot like the one he'd fallen in love with at the Miller's.

Today as Tommy smoothed the photograph on the wall, he remembered how it had felt to touch a real airplane. "The next time I get that close," he murmured, "I'll get a ride no matter what." He could still hear George saying, "Come to Pittsburgh, and I'll make him pay up." Tommy didn't know yet how he'd get there. Pap would need more cooling-off time before Tommy could even mention the promise to him.

A slamming of car doors told of the return of the

picnickers. Tommy listened to the confusion of noises that began below. Ma's empty salad bowls and cake plates rattled as she carried them to the kitchen. Pap bumped around in his room, changing his clothes before tackling the evening chores. And feet clattering up the stairs announced Mark before he burst into the bedroom.

"Hey, Tommy, you sure missed a good picnic! And Rachel Cranby got mighty sad when she heard you weren't coming."

Tommy threw his pillow at the grin on his brother's face. "It's not Mrs. Cranby's *daughter* I'm interested in, Cupid, it's her *cooking*. If you forgot my cake..." He grabbed the bundle that Mark pulled from under his shirt.

Mark tugged off the knickers he wore for church and stepped into worn overalls. "Thank Mrs. Miller for the rest of it. She caught me wrapping your cake in a Sunday School paper. First she gives me the dickens for using the Lord's Word that way. Then she puts the cake into one of her own napkins and throws in 'a few other things.' I could hardly get the darned thing under my shirt!"

Tommy spread the napkin open on his bed. Under the first fold lay a huge chunk of baked ham nestled between two thick, well-buttered slices of fresh bread. Beneath another fold were two crusty-brown chicken legs. A half-dozen fat oatmeal cookies tumbled forth next, and the last corner revealed an enormous slice of devil's food cake.

Mark bounced excitedly on his bed. "Got some interesting news for you, too."

"Well, it will have to wait." Tommy stuffed a cookie into his mouth as he rewrapped the rest of the smuggled feast. He retrieved his pillow and arranged it to conceal the bulging napkin. "If we don't get busy, Pap will have us cleaning all the barn stalls tomorrow—Sunday or not."

Later, as the boys carried froth-topped buckets of milk into the springhouse, Mark asked, "Ever hear of a magazine called *Aero*, Tommy?"

Tommy shook his head. "*Saturday Evening Post* and *Youth's Companion*'s about all I know. Why?"

"Mrs. Beatley—you know, the old postmaster's wife? —she mentioned *Aero* when the folks were talking about the barnstormers."

Tommy winced with regret. There had been flying talk at the picnic and he had missed it! "Well, tell me about it. What did everybody say?"

"Oh, you know. The ones that took a ride were bragging about how they weren't the least bit afraid. And the ones that didn't fly were saying they'd go when they could keep one foot on the ground. Mrs. Parrish started bragging about getting an air mail letter from her sister in New York. She said it came as far as Philadelphia on that airplane service they started last spring.

"That's when Mrs. Beatley chimed in. 'My late husband anticipated that airships would be used by the postal service,' she says. 'He was quite anxious to learn all that he could about aeronautics. He even subscribed to a periodical on the subject.'"

Tommy had to laugh at Mark's accurate imitation of Mrs. Beatley.

"A——" Mark continued in his own voice, "Mrs.

Beatley said that Mr. Beatley'd saved copies of that magazine, the one called *Aero*, clear from 1910. Now that she's moving, she can't take them along. She was asking if anyone wanted them."

Tommy's stomach turned over. "Who got them, Mark? Who'd she give them to?"

"Mr. Burvin said he supposed he could lay them around in his barbershop. I said maybe you'd like some of them. But Pap said you did enough daydreaming. I think Ma was going to take them 'til Pap said that. Then she said she guessed it was better to keep your mind on practical things."

Tommy's hands shook as he emptied his buckets into the milkcans standing in the cool spring water. How could his parents have done it? Hadn't there ever been a time in their lives when they had had a dream? What was so wrong about dreaming, if you also worked to make it come true?

"Well, practical or not, I'm going to keep on dreaming." The words helped dissolve the hard lump in Tommy's throat. "And tomorrow I'm going to the barbershop!"

Several weeks later, Mr. Burvin looked up and smiled as Tommy came into his shop. He nudged the customer in his chair. "Hey, John, whatcha think of a boy who comes to the barbershop two, three times a week—just to read the magazines?"

John Willis's eyes twinkled above the foam on his face. "It hasn't been all that long ago that I did the same thing, Glenn. At least until my ma caught on."

"Oh, he ain't looking at girlie magazines. He only has

time for them ones about flying machines." Mr. Burvin raised his voice. "Keep on, son, and you'll soon be building your own airplane—and selling rides in it." He chuckled. "Ol' John here'll be your first customer."

"Not likely, Glenn! I got enough troubles with these dang automobiles. Sure was a lot simpler when a livery stable just took care of horses."

Tommy smiled, wondering if Mr. Burvin knew how close to the truth his teasing came. An airplane of his own was just what Tommy dreamed of, day and night. Maybe he *would* end up building one someday. He settled into a back corner and began to read.

A short time later Tommy's attention was caught by frantic motions from the doorway. He looked around him at empty chairs, then walked forward. "Were you waving at me, Miss Bronson?"

"Yes, Tommy. I need your help." She took a deep breath. "I have searched all over this town for Mr. Willis. Now I find him in a place no lady can enter. Please ask him to return to his place of business. I must find out what's wrong with my automobile."

Tommy glanced over his shoulder. Mr. Willis and Mr. Burvin were well into their afternoon checker game. It seemed a shame to interrupt them. Especially when there was no need. "Miss Bronson, I know a little bit about cars. Would you mind if I took a look at yours?"

"I would be delighted if *someone* would. I'll be late for my literary meeting, and I'm to provide the refreshments. Come along."

Tommy had to step lively to match her speed. "I knew something was wrong when I was driving to work this morning." she told him. "The machine seemed to be running with great difficulty. It almost stopped as I came over the Knob."

Tommy heard this with interest. Of course, when a car faltered going uphill, it could mean a lot of things, but he had a hunch. He stopped at the librarian's elderly Oldsmobile and lifted the hood—then gave a satisfied nod. John Willis could finish his checker game in peace.

"Here's your trouble." He pointed to one of the spark plugs. "See that little wire that's loose? It needs to be screwed back under here." He replaced the wire under a small nut as he spoke. . . . "Let's see if that fixed it."

Together they drove out to the steep hill at the edge of town. Without a pause the ancient car conquered the sharp grade, its owner beaming with delight.

They had turned around and were driving back down Main Street when Miss Bronson exclaimed, "Tommy, you're a genius!" Before Tommy could protest, she added, "Oh *ho!*" and swung into the curb. Her sharp eyes had fixed on Mr. Willis, just leaving the barber-shop.

"So you finally come out, John Willis! Well, I don't need you now—I've found a fine mechanic. You should hire him. Then there'd be someone around when your garage is supposed to be open." Miss Bronson rummaged in her purse. "What's the charge, Tommy?"

Tommy climbed down, shaking his head. "Not a thing, ma'am. Glad I could help."

Miss Bronson nodded. "Very well—I owe you a favor." She drove away, her final, "Thank you so much," drifting back on the hot afternoon air.

"Now what the devil was that all about?" Mr. Willis asked.

Tommy shrugged. "Oh, nothing, Mr. Willis. Miss Bronson's just happy because she won't miss her literary meeting. She thought something terrible was wrong with her car. Turned out to be just a spark plug wire."

Mr. Willis studied Tommy. "You can fix more than loose wires, though, can't you? I remember—your pa was saying at the church picnic that you fixed his car. Clyde Miller said you'd replaced a head gasket."

Tommy was too surprised to answer. Imagine Pap bragging to folks about his fixing job when he'd never said beans to him!

Mr. Willis stroked at his freshly shaved chin. "Maybe Miss Bronson has an idea there. It'd sure be nice to have some free time I could count on. These fool cars always need something at the craziest hours."

He glanced up and spoke so abruptly that Tommy jumped. "Well, boy, what do you think? Want to help me out?"

"I . . . I . . ." Tommy was so excited he stammered. "I sure do, Mr. Willis."

"You still in school?"

"Not right now, sir. Summer vacation's a couple more weeks. And I'm sure I could get out of school to work afternoons."

"Well, we can try it. . . . Where you headed now?"

Tommy glanced at the sun. "I guess it's time to get on home. But Pap doesn't question where I go afternoons, so long as I do my chores."

"Then you come by early tomorrow afternoon. I'll show you what I want done."

"Yes, *sir*, Mr. Willis! . . . I sure do appreciate the chance."

Mr. Willis hitched at a suspender. "Hmph. Showing's better than telling, son. We'll see how you do." He walked off down the dusty street.

Tommy turned toward the doorway of the barbershop. Mr. Burvin stood there grinning. "You oughta see your face. I doubt Elijah looked any happier when he saw the heavenly chariot coming." The barber held out several copies of *Aero*. "Better carry these home. You won't have time to read here no more."

Dazed, Tommy accepted the magazines in silence.

"And, Tommy," Mr. Burvin drawled. "You might want to inquire what John's planning to pay you. I hear those airplanes cost a pretty penny." He winked, then turned back to lock the shop door.

Chapter

4

TOMMY CHOSE A PAIR OF LONG JOHNS FROM THE ONES piled in his drawer and gave the cigar box tucked beneath them a satisfied pat. His pay from working in the garage almost filled the box now. He'd soon have to ask Mr. Shipley, the druggist, for another. He wished he had time to sit down and count his savings again. But Mark was waiting.

As the two boys trudged to school through the season's first light snow, Tommy hardly noticed Mark's unusual silence. He was thinking about the library book he carried inside the protection of his coat.

Miss Bronson had found it for him. He didn't know how she had learned of his interest in airplanes. Suddenly one afternoon, she had appeared at the garage, looking very pleased with herself as she said, "Well now, Mr. Davison, I've come to repay your favor!"

Tommy had had to think for a moment to realize what she meant. It had been months since he'd fixed that wire on her car. Miss Bronson had laughed at his puzzled look. "Oh, I know I've been a long time about it, but this wasn't easy to get. There aren't many books about aeronautics, you know."

She had chattered on, seeming not to notice that Tommy couldn't take his eyes off the large volume she held in her white-gloved hands. "It's high time the library owned a book on aviation, so I ordered this one. I thought it was only fair that you should have first chance at it. But, mercy, you can't touch it with those greasy hands! Come by after work, and we'll check it out to you properly."

In the four weeks that he had been allowed to keep it, Tommy had read and reread the book in every spare minute. Now the precious time was up, and the book must be returned this morning. Tommy paused at the library steps. "Coming in, Mark?"

"No, I . . . I'll go on ahead." They had not been walking very fast, but Mark was almost panting. For the first time Tommy noticed that the flush on his brother's face was deeper than normal.

"Hey, Mark, you feeling all right?"

"Just that old sore throat. I'll be okay."

Tommy watched his brother plod on toward the school. Walking that slow and talking that little sure wasn't like Mark. "Maybe I'd better tell Ma how he's acting," Tommy murmured.

It was nearly time for the lunch bell when Mark's teacher sent for Tommy. Young Miss Fitzgerald, who'd been Tommy's teacher the year before, was known for her pleasant smile. But when Tommy entered the room, her face was very serious. She fiddled nervously with the watch pinned to her white shirtwaist.

"Tommy, I'm afraid I made a mistake in not sending for you sooner. So many of the children have had colds —I thought Mark just needed to rest a bit."

She gestured toward the coat room. Mark was inside, on a cot provided for what the pupils called "sickers and fakers." He lay quite still, his face now almost purplish. Tommy heard at once the cause of Miss Fitzgerald's concern. Mark was uttering a strange rasping noise, as he struggled for each breath.

"He just began to breathe that way," Miss Fitzgerald whispered. She bit her lip. "I think you'd better find Doctor McNally."

Tommy rushed out onto Main Street without bothering to go back for his coat. Mark's noisy breathing kept echoing in his ears. It was a terrifying sound! How could Mark have become so sick in such a short time?

Thankfulness welled up in Tommy as he raced into the side street and saw that Doc's car was in its place under the leafless lilac bush. He took the front steps in one leap and thumped on the front door.

"All right, I'm coming!" Doc, his glasses resting as usual atop his thinning white hair, opened the door. A lunch napkin hung from his top vest buttonhole. "There's no need to knock the place down," he grumbled.

"I'm sorry, Dr. McNally, but Mark's real sick. Can you come to the school right away? He's breathing awful funny."

The stout little doctor peered closely at Tommy's

worried face, then reached for his bag. He called back over his shoulder, "Margaret, I have to go to the school. Tell the afternoon patients I'll be back as soon as I can." He lifted his coat from the hall tree—replacing it with his napkin—and followed Tommy out the door.

Classes had been dismissed for lunch, but a group of town children stood near the school doorway. Dr. McNally frowned fiercely and pointed a finger at them. "You! There's nothing you can do here but get in the way. Now, get on home, all of you, before your mothers start to worry." He hurried on into the building.

Miss Fitzgerald was bent over Mark, applying a damp cloth to his forehead. She started and drew back, as if afraid that she might be doing the wrong thing. Mark's breathing had become even more labored, and there was a foreign odor in the cramped, unventilated room. Each time Mark struggled for air, Tommy strained for breath with him. If only he really could help his brother breathe!

Doctor McNally's face was grave when he looked up from inspecting Mark's throat. "I'll need to get this boy to my surgery at once." He reached for the quilt that lay at Mark's feet and wrapped it carefully around his patient. His eyes met Tommy's as he bent to lift the head of the cot. "Pick up that end, son. There's no time to lose."

The short walk down Main Street was a nightmare. Whispering people stepped aside to let them pass with their strange burden. Tommy finally understood a word that had been murmured several times—"*diphtheria*." Several who heard it drew back fearfully. Mrs. Burvin hurried her two small children to the other side of the street.

"Doc never said that," Tommy thought angrily. "It

can't be that. Why, Mark could die!" He stumbled as they passed over the threshold of the side door that led into Doc's surgery, then caught himself and lowered his end of the cot.

"Easy now, Tommy. Let's get him on the table." Doc was already lifting Mark's shoulders. His wife, Margaret, who was also his nurse, came from the waiting room and helped them move Mark from the cot. While Doc turned to the sink to scrub his hands, Margaret McNally took the sick boy's pulse and studied the unhealthy color of his face. Not fear, but a tense experience showed in her lined face as she listened to the dreadful sawing sound of Mark's breathing.

"Go quickly, Tommy. Get your father." She shook her head as Tommy started to speak. "No, I can help here. We won't need you. But your parents will have to know."

Tommy glanced at the doctor. He had opened a small rectangular case and was selecting a medium-sized tube from the variety within. His movements were swift but unflustered as he attached the tube to a slender, curved instrument.

Mrs. McNally tucked the quilt so that it held Mark's arms tight to his sides, then moved to take a firm grip on the patient's head. As Tommy hurried out she said, "It will be all right. But hurry!"

An hour later, Tommy sat in Dr. McNally's waiting room. His mother had been holding tightly to his hand ever since they had arrived in town. He was dimly aware that his fingers hurt, but most of his mind was concentrated on the next room.

It had seemed to take forever to get home, even with the ride Mr. Willis had insisted on giving him. Worst of all, Pap and the car were gone when they got there. Ma didn't know for sure where. All they could do then was leave Pap a note—and thank Heaven for Mr. Willis's kindness. And all they could do now was pray while they waited.

Finally Margaret McNally reappeared and beckoned to them. They stood up and followed her into the surgery. Mark still lay on the table, but his breathing seemed quieter. Mrs. Davison stiffened as she saw the white cloths that lay around Mark's neck. The doctor took her hand in both of his and spoke gently. "Now, Emma, don't get excited. The worst is over, and I think he'll be all right. I had to perform an entubation. I just inserted a little tube into his throat so he could breathe better. He seems to be holding his own now." The doctor looked around. "But where's Bert?"

Tommy's mother lowered her eyes. "I don't know. He may have gone up to Foss Conner's place."

Tommy winced with shame. Foss Conner! No wonder Ma hadn't wanted to tell him. Foss was said to make the best moonshine whiskey in this county. Not often, but once in a while, it seemed Pap just had to go buy some. When he did, he was a long time getting home and a good bit poorer when he got there.

Doc nodded in tired understanding. "Well then, I'll just have to discuss this with you. Come and sit down." Still holding her hand, he led her over to sit with him on a nearby couch. "You see, Emma, Mark is very ill. It's diphtheria." Mrs. Davison gasped. "Now, now, I know that's a frightening word, but I didn't lie to you. I do think he's going to be all right. But he's going to need serum and special care for a while. That's why I want to send him over to the hospital in Middleton right away. Tommy can go over to the funeral parlor and fetch the ambulance."

Tommy's mother suddenly covered her face with her hands and began to weep. She made no sound; the awful tears just appeared, trickling through her fingers.

"Here now, Emma," Doc spoke in surprise. "Don't you believe me? I think Mark will be fine."

Mrs. Davison raised her head and whispered, "I believe you. But I can't send him to a hospital. We haven't any money." She struggled to speak with dignity. "We had a little put by. But today, when I looked in the . . . the place where we keep it, it was gone. Every bit of it." Her face twisted with fear. "The hospital won't take Mark without money!"

Suddenly Tommy was on his feet. "Don't worry about it, Ma. We got money. I've saved every cent I earned from Mr. Willis. You can use that—as much as you need. You go ahead and fix up whatever you have to, Doc. I'll get the ambulance."

He was out the surgery door before they could speak —and before they could see the tears in his eyes. Well, so what! Even a man could cry if his brother was sick enough to be almost dying. That's all it was.

He certainly wasn't crying over his money. Even if he was pretty sure his parents could never pay back what he'd give them. What did it matter that he'd have to start all over on saving for his airplane? Only a little kid would cry for a reason like that. He felt a million years old as he hurried down the street.

Chapter

5

"POW!" THE EXPLOSIVE SOUND FROM THE STREET MADE Tommy stop working. He listened, puzzled, as several more explosions echoed through the quiet garage. The end of December was certainly too late in the year for anyone to have leftover Fourth of July firecrackers. Was someone still celebrating the Armistice?

Finally, curiosity won. Tommy slid out from under Mr. Wiley's Oakland and stood up. Wiping his greasy hands on a rag, he opened the garage door and looked around.

The source of the noise was not hard to find. An ancient automobile was panting down the street. Tommy was almost certain that at one time it had been a Model T or, more likely, several of them. The headlights, though, were from a yellow Hudson and one front fender looked as if it had originally belonged to a blue Buick.

Most incredible was the long truck body that had been welded onto the back and was supported by two sets of rear wheels. Years ago the truck bed and cab had been painted a vivid green and trimmed with elaborate gold scrolls. On the door that Tommy could see, peeling gold letters spelled out:

CAPTAIN MICHAEL KELLY
World's Most Daring Pilot
Amazing Aerobatic Feats!

This fantastic vehicle produced one more backfire— the loudest of all—and came to a stop. Its lanky driver stood up and leaped over his door onto the street. He patted the blue fender. "Never mind, old girl, you done your best." He looked up and down the frozen slush that was Main Street. "Well, we almost made it to civilization."

Tommy stepped forward. "Anything I can do to help, mister?"

The man was older than his easy exit from the truck had made him seem. His hair, though clipped very short, was gray, and the many wrinkles on his thin face owed as much to the years as to hours of direct sunlight. Even in midwinter his face was tanned enough to fade the blue of his eyes.

While Tommy studied him, the man studied the sign above Tommy's head. Just last week Mr. Willis had grudgingly added a small *And Garage* to the large black letters that spelled out WILLIS LIVERY STABLE. The man closed one eye and tugged at his veined, red nose.

"Well, son, if she was a horse, the only kind thing would be to shoot her. But old Bessie here will live again, once I have some time to work on her. Your boss around, boy?"

"He's gone home for supper. Ought to be back before long."

"Well, my name's Zeb." The man held out a large, roughened hand. When Tommy offered his own name and hand, Zeb smiled down at the traces of black dirt caught under the nails and in the creases of their fingers. "Looks like you've worked on a few engines yourself."

Zeb glanced back over his shoulder at the truck. "I reckon I can't leave Bessie sitting here in the street. Is there some place I can push her to?"

"Yes sir. We can put her on the vacant lot behind the garage. Lots of times Mr. Willis puts a car there until we can get to it."

Zeb's eyes narrowed with interest. "Work gets kind of piled up sometimes, does it? Now that's a right hopeful sign. Might be your Mr. Willis could use some help. Least it won't do no harm to ask, eh son?"

It wasn't long before Mr. Willis returned from supper, and Tommy went back to repairing the Oakland. But he couldn't help being interested in the fragments of conversation that drifted over from where the two men stood talking in the doorway.

"Can't pay you much," Mr. Willis was saying just as Tommy finished his work.

"... A place to sleep and grub 'til I prove myself," Zeb replied.

Tommy got to his feet and glanced at the clock above the garage office. It was time to clean up his tools and start for home. With reluctance he began to place wrenches and pliers into their proper storage boxes. Having heard this much of the conversation, he found it hard to leave without knowing the outcome.

"... No spare room ...," Mr. Willis was mumbling.

"Cot in the garage ... do fine," Zeb drawled.

Tommy hadn't realized how much he wanted Zeb to stay until he heard Mr. Willis's decision. "Well, I don't see how I can refuse a deal like that, if you're satisfied." A sudden rush of happiness spread through him as the two men shook hands. Tommy had a feeling that Zeb needed this job. It wasn't natural to be as thin as he was.

But Tommy had to admit to himself that most of his joy was selfish. Earlier, when they had moved the truck to the back lot, Zeb had gestured toward a bulky, canvas-covered object in the truck bed. "If you like working on engines, Tom, there's one that'll drive you crazy. That OX-5 runs like a dream until it gets about five hundred feet in the air. Then it just conks out cold."

Tommy's eyes had widened into a stare. A real airplane engine! He had been opening his mouth to ask about the sign on the truck door when Mr. Willis had returned.

Now Tommy finished cleaning up and called a cheerful "Good night!" to the two men. He needn't hang around to catch Zeb tonight. There'd be lots of time for questions if Zeb was going to stay on.

And he did stay on. Weeks passed, good weeks, for Mark was gradually getting well again, and Tommy, by watching and questioning Zeb, was learning more and more about airplanes, as well as cars.

Tommy only wished he could talk with Ma about

money as easily as he talked with Zeb about motors. He knew she worried about paying him back. She didn't say much until one night when she was fixing Mark's supper tray. Then she said, "Tommy, I feel so bad about your savings. I've been going over the accounts with your pa, hoping we could start to pay you back. But he's right—this is no time of year to squeeze out extra cash. There won't be any 'til the new crops come in."

"That's okay, Ma," Tommy answered, not looking at her. He fiddled with Mark's salt shaker. If only he could tell her his feelings! He wanted to say, "We got Mark home with his breathing all quiet and even. And his face is back to a color that doesn't scare us half to death. That's enough for me. I *been* paid back." He wanted to say it, but he couldn't. It just sounded too highfalutin'. Instead he muttered, "I can earn more," and picked up the tray to carry it upstairs.

Mark began his questions as soon as he heard Tommy's feet on the top step. "What did Zeb tell you today? Did he finish the story about Captain Kelly's feud with that bunch of exhibition pilots?"

Tommy laughed. "You ought to know by now, Mark, Zeb never *finishes* a story. But I did hear how Zeb got the crowd away from those parachute jumpers." He shook his head as Mark settled back onto his pillows. "Oh no, you don't. No more telling stories to you while my own supper gets cold. You eat, and I'll eat, and then I'll be back up to tell you all about it."

Tommy turned in the doorway. "You might want to figure this out. Zeb told folks that jumping from a plane *with* a parachute was nothing. He said he'd jump without one!" Laughing at Mark's expression, Tommy ran down the stairs. He joined his parents at the supper table and dug into the food heaped on his plate.

Suddenly Mr. Davison pushed back his chair. He glared at his wife and demanded, "Well, Emma, did you show Tommy them eggs?"

Tommy's mother jumped, then faltered, "Why, no, Bert. There's hardly been time."

Tommy's father slammed his large hand down flat on the table, spinning a teaspoon onto the floor. " 'Course you haven't had time. And if you had time, you couldn't a found him. He ain't never around when you need him, and when he does do anything, he only half does it."

Tommy studied his father with bewilderment. There had been a change in him these last months. At first he'd seemed proud about Tommy's job in town—not that he'd ever come right out and said so. But since Mark's illness, Mr. Davison had taken to complaining about Tommy's absences.

"Six eggs I found in the chicken yard," his father was saying now. "*Six*. After you were s'posed to have gathered them."

Tommy flushed and gazed down at his fork. He'd been pretty tired last night. Not until he took on half of Mark's chores as well as his own had he realized how much his brother did around the farm. Last night, just at dusk, Tommy had gathered the eggs in the nest boxes, but he'd decided to leave hunting for the ones in the yard 'til the morning. Then he'd forgotten to go back.

"I'm sorry, Pap. I did check the yard this afternoon, but I didn't find any."

" 'Course you didn't! 'Cause I already done the job for you. No wonder I can't make no money off this farm.

I have to do my work and finish yours too. It ain't possible for a man to run a farm this size alone."

"I'm sure Tommy won't forget again, Bert," Mrs. Davison put in quickly. "How about a nice piece of dried apple pie now?"

"You're sure he won't forget again, are you?" Pap mimicked in a nasty tone. "Well, *I* ain't. I got no time to sit eating pie. I got to go check to see what else he's left half done."

The slam of the kitchen door echoed in their ears as Tommy and his mother stared at each other. They spoke together.

"He's not been feeling so good lately. Don't pay him no mind."

"I won't forget again, Ma. Don't worry."

A helpless churning in his stomach, Tommy tried to think what else he could say that might erase the distress on Ma's face. Into their silence dropped a vigorous pounding from the ceiling above. Tommy rose from the table, a grin starting on his lips.

"Mark's feeling mighty lively. I'd better get on up there before he decides to slide down the banister."

Relieved, he saw his mother's face brighten. Whatever was troubling Pap, they had faced and come through a lot worse in the past weeks. Now was no time to forget their blessings.

THE SHORT STALK OF CRABGRASS ON WHICH HE HAD BEEN chewing fell from Mark's open mouth. "You mean, Zeb's boss was a woman!" he gasped.

Tommy shifted his seat on the woodpile. "Well, at first Captain Kelly and his wife ran the show together. Then one day when the Captain was carrying cans of gas back from town, a car hit and killed him. Zeb says Mrs. Kelly made two vows right then: she'd keep the show going as long as she could—and she'd never ask anyone to do something she wouldn't do herself . . . Remember when I told you about that stunt Zeb thought up—where he jumped from an airplane without a parachute?"

"Yeah, you said he landed in a big pile of hay right in front of the grandstand."

"Right. Well, Zeb told me the other day that it was

Mrs. Kelly who told him it didn't look dangerous enough. That's when she tried climbing down onto the landing gear and hanging by her knees, then dropping head first into the hay pile. Zeb said he could hardly refuse to do it that way after a woman had done it first."

"But they could get killed! That's crazy!" Mark shook his head in disbelief.

Tommy laughed. "Zeb says you have to be crazy to work in a flying show. But they have two kinds of crazy people, he told me. Some are like him—danged fools that will try anything just to see if they can do it and live to tell about it. Then, there's the other ones. They don't like doing the stunts, but they're crazy about airplanes. They'll do anything to earn enough to pay for a ship and fill its gas tank. If they have some left over for food and a bed for themselves, they figure they're rich!'"

Mark slid down from his perch and beat sawdust from the seat of his overalls. "Well, it sure is a darn silly way to live! I'll take farming any day." He gathered up an armload of logs and trudged away toward the house.

Tommy watched until Mark disappeared among the trees that were just beginning to show new leaf buds. He envied the way his brother accepted being a farmer. As Mark grew stronger each day, he threw himself into the farm chores without complaint. And it wasn't just that Mark was happy to be free from his sick bed. He really *liked* what they had to do. Mark enjoyed farming so much he couldn't understand people who would choose something else.

But Tommy could. Sometimes just thinking about spending the rest of his life cleaning out chicken coops, butchering hogs, and spreading manure on the fields could make him feel miserable. It wasn't so much that the work was hard and dirty. He worked just as hard and got even dirtier at the garage. And he never minded that. Working with machinery was different. There was a pleasure for him in cleaning, adjusting, and repairing a motor that he knew he'd never find in hoeing a cornfield.

"And even if I didn't get my airplane ride, I still know how those pilots feel," he murmured. "I'd sure trade a soft bed and a few meals if I could get the chance to fly."

The sun shining into his eyes brought Tommy out of his reverie. He jumped down and at top speed gathered a large armload of wood. I'd better make tracks for town, he was thinking. This is the day Zeb said I could finish up on the OX-5 engine, if we get that universal joint on Mr. Burvin's Ford fixed.

Turning into the garage, Tommy went straight to the corner where the Burvin car sat waiting. He had expected to see Zeb's feet protruding from under the rear bumper. Instead, he heard Zeb's soft drawl coming from the tiny closet John Willis used as an office.

"Time for me to be moving on, John. The fellas are rarin' to get the show started up again, and they'll need me."

John Willis's deep rumble replied, "I surely do hate to see you go, Zeb. Folks around here been real pleased with your work. This would be a good town for you to settle down in."

Zeb chuckled. "You know old tramps like me can't never settle down. We got to keep movin' so the moss don't grow on us."

Mr. Willis glanced up as Tommy appeared in the

doorway. Instead of offering his usual friendly nod, Tommy's employer looked depressed. "Well, Tom," he said with a resigned sigh, "looks like you and me are back to running the shop by ourselves. Better start telling the customers about that garage in Middleton again."

Zeb raised a hand in protest. "I don't know as you'll have to turn business away, John. This boy's been mighty quick to learn what I could teach him. You'd best let him handle whatever he says he can."

At any other time Tommy would have been delighted by the unexpected compliment. But now he was too shaken by the news that Zeb was leaving. "Will you have to go soon, Zeb?" he asked, trying to keep his voice from cracking.

"Well son, it's like this." Zeb ran a hand through his short gray hair. "Now that the war's over, Miz Kelly's pilots are gettin' discharged and coming back to the show. There's other fliers drifting in, too—all of them just itchin' to show what they can do in those surplus planes they're buyin' off the government." He held up an envelope. "I got a letter from Miz Kelly just yesterday. She says she needs me to work on the airplanes. If I'm not there to help, some of them greenhorns are liable to fasten the wings onto the crates the planes come in!"

Zeb paused, but for once Tommy didn't laugh at his foolishness. The mechanic glanced down and away. "So I reckon I'll be leavin' early tomorrow," he mumbled.

Late that afternoon, Tommy stood watching Zeb gather together his few belongings and stow them in the ancient green truck. Together they lifted the OX-5 into the truck bed, and Tommy helped Zeb pack rolled cardboard and old rags around it until they were sure it would not slide or scratch against the truck's sides.

With affection, Tommy patted the rebuilt engine. It had taught him a lot. Zeb finished tying the canvas over it, then stared down at the bundle.

"Well," he said, "we done our best with her. But I ain't takin' no bets that she won't quit cold again in the middle of a climb-out."

The garage was filling with shadows when Zeb offered his hand to Tommy. "We'd best say good-bye now, Tom. I'll be leavin' early." He glanced ruefully toward the front of the truck." "Coulda started tonight, had I got around to fixing them headlights. But at least I got the old heap runnin' pretty good."

Tommy hoped Zeb didn't hear the hard swallow he had to make to clear his throat. "I'll miss you, Zeb. And I thank you for all you've taught me."

"Don't mention it, son, don't mention it." Zeb patted Tommy's shoulder, and Tommy thought it sounded as if Zeb had had to swallow hard too. "We're friends, you and me. Friends just naturally help each other. Git goin' now, before your folks get upset that you ain't home. It's near dark already." He gave Tommy a gentle push toward the door and muttered low, "I'll miss you, too."

Tommy had to hurry to make it along his shortcut through the woods before the path under the trees disappeared in the darkness. So many feelings were churning inside of him that he forgot to watch out for the fat tree root that marked the place where the path emerged onto his father's back field. He went sprawling as his toe caught under it. A moment later he was back on his feet and sprinting toward the lights that beckoned from the windows of home.

Pap would be mad and Ma would be worried because he'd missed supper. But maybe when they heard about Zeb, they'd understand. And wouldn't they be proud when they heard what Zeb had said about him to Mr. Willis!

Tommy finished telling his parents about all that had happened that day at the same time he finished the food Ma had kept warm for him. "I'll have to work longer hours, so that's more money," he explained. "And I think maybe Mr. Willis will give me a raise. Zeb was making more than me. If I'm going to do his job, stands to reason I ought to get his pay."

"Stands to reason, does it?" The words erupting from Mr. Davison were hot with suppressed anger. "And who do you 'reason' is going to help me here, while you're playing mechanic at that garage?"

"Why . . . Mark . . ." Tommy stammered.

"Boy, don't you even know what time of year it is? Don't you see them crocuses coming up in your Ma's garden, and the birds starting to build in the eaves of the barn? It's planting time! I need you *and* Mark to get all done that we got to do this spring. I can't spare you no more, now the slack season's over."

"But, Pap . . ."

"But, Pap, nothing! You tell John Willis your pa needs you to home now. He'll just have to get along without you."

Tommy felt the tears that were forming in his eyes and blinked them away while he tried to think. "Look, Pap, how about this? You know that fellow they call Smiley? Mrs. Beatley and some of the ladies used to hire him every spring to work their gardens. Well, he was in the garage today. Said he didn't have hardly any work. Mrs. Beatley's moved, and some of the others are doing their own gardening. I bet we could get him to come help out. He doesn't charge much—I could pay him out of what I make."

"I wouldn't have that half-wit working any farm of mine. He can't even talk plain. I'd be spending all day trying to figure out what he was saying."

"You can understand him, Pap. You just have to talk slow and let him talk slow back."

Pap's face was getting red. "I told you, I won't have him on the place! Now you quit your sassin' and get on out there to your chores or I'm going to take my belt to you. The idea! Here you are, so crazy about the place that will be yours someday, you're willing to hire a moron to farm it for you!"

"He's not a moron, Pap. Miss Fitzgerald says he's just a little retarded."

Pap jumped up. "I told you—*not another word!* So long as I've got two able-bodied sons to help me, there'll be no hired hands on this farm. Now you move!"

Tommy clenched his fists, then swung around and flung open the kitchen door. He let it bang hard behind him.

Chapter

7

NO BIRD HAD CHIRPED, AND THERE WAS NOT A HINT OF dawn light in the bedroom when Tommy awoke. He pulled the covers around his shoulders and lay staring into the darkness, aroused by the angry thoughts that had followed him to bed and allowed him only a short, fitful slumber. "Pap is just plain mean. He knows how I love working at the garage. He just can't stand it that I have a chance to get away from this blame farm."

Tommy's hands pulled at the quilt that they gripped. He heard a soft *r-r-rip* as a few of its ancient stitches parted. He rolled onto his other side. "It isn't as if Pap doesn't have help. Mark's able to keep up with anyone now. And I even offered to pay Smiley!"

Tommy attacked his pillow with several vicious punches. "It would all have worked out fine, if Pap hadn't decided to get stubborn. That's Pap—he expects a man's work from you, but don't you dare start think-ing like a man. Don't ever start making plans for your own life. Pap wants to do all your planning for you."

Suddenly Tommy sat up, remembering the final thought he'd had before he dropped off last night. ". . . Maybe the only way to do what I want *is* to get away from Pap." A curious, leaping sensation passed through Tommy's stomach as he considered the idea. Imagine having whole *days* to call his own!

"I'm so tired of trying to do all he wants and still have a couple hours for myself! And if I stay here, I won't even have that time anymore," he muttered. "Pap's set on running every single minute of my life."

With one determined thrust, Tommy threw back the quilts and swung his legs over the edge of the bed. He shivered as his bare feet hit the floorboards, but his mind was too busy to care. "I'm going to do it!" he vowed. "I'm getting out of here!"

As if in answer, a small shaft of bright moonlight thrust through the dormer window and spotlighted the clothes that he had hung on his bedpost the night before. He dressed in minutes. Pulling his pillow out of its case and dropping it onto the bed, he tiptoed across to his dresser. He inched a drawer open and began to pull out clothes and cram them into the empty pillowcase.

He smiled at how carefully he opened a second drawer. Why was he being so quiet, anyway? Mark probably wouldn't wake up if the whole dresser fell over. But, now that Tommy's mind was made up, he wouldn't take a chance on having to answer a lot of questions.

For a moment Tommy paused and looked toward his brother. He sure was going to miss Mark. But, sooner or later, a man had to follow his own ideas, even if he had to leave home to do it. "Just you wait 'til I come back, Mark," he whispered. "I'll have some stories for you that will make Zeb's sound tame."

Now that he'd said Zeb's name aloud, Tommy knew he'd had his friend in mind all along. That was why he'd awakened so early. If he hurried, he could probably catch Zeb before he left. Tommy reached far back into the drawer for his cigar box. Tucking it under his arm and tossing the pillowcase across his shoulder, he started down the stairs.

When Tommy opened the outside door in the deserted kitchen, bright moonlight fell across the threshold. He hesitated, then turned back to place the cigar box on the kitchen table. Opening the box lid, he pulled out a small handful of bills and stuffed them into his coat pocket. Then he flipped the lid closed and pushed the box across to a spot in front of Pap's empty chair. "There, Pap," he murmured, "I said I'd pay for a man to help in my place, and I will."

Glancing at the vacant seat at the other end of the table, Tommy whispered, "I'll be back, Ma. Don't worry about me." He straightened his shoulders, pulled his heavy collar up around his ears, and eased the kitchen door shut behind him. The pillowcase jounced on his shoulder as he settled into a long, rapid stride for the walk into town.

Zeb was sitting on the edge of his cot, just beginning to dress, when Tommy entered the garage. "Wal, Tommy boy," he said, his eyes still sleepy. "I thought we said our good-bys last night."

"I've decided I don't want to say good-by, Zeb," Tommy answered. "I'd like to come with you."

Zeb started to open his mouth, then closed it again. Tommy was reminded of the time a while back when a customer had asked what Zeb's last name was. The mechanic had answered, with a cool stare, "I never ask questions about a man's personal business. What he wants you to know, he'll tell you." Tommy wondered if Zeb would hold to that principle now.

Standing up, Zeb began to scratch up and down each side of his red undershirt, while he looked thoughtful. After long minutes, he spoke. "I'd be glad for your company, and that's a fact. It's a long ride," he said, "and Lord knows I could use another mechanic to help me when I get there." He studied Tommy's face. Tommy's eyes met his without wavering. Zeb stuck out his hand. "Sure, come along, son. But don't come crying to me when you find out the world out there ain't perfect neither."

The sun was going down behind the Kentucky hills when Zeb spoke—his voice loud to carry over the noise of the truck. "I reckon the Franklin Fairgrounds ought to be pretty close now. I can smell the fumes from the planes."

Tommy straightened and realized that he, too, could detect an oily, not really unpleasant odor drifting above the scent of blossoming trees and spring flowers. He smiled over at Zeb. "I won't be sorry to get there," he shouted.

Zeb nodded. "Sure will feel good to sleep stretched full out with somethin' over our heads," he yelled back.

"I feel like my body's got a perm'nant curve from trying to curl around that durn engine."

Tommy's sympathy was tinged with guilt, since he had been spending the nights in the truck's cab. But Zeb had insisted that the truck seat was too short for him to sleep on anyway.

"Ouch!" Tommy yelped as the truck splashed into and through a shallow creek bed, throwing him sideways against the door frame. He made a face at the brown grit that clung to his fingers after he'd rubbed the side of his head.

"Sorry, Tom. Couldn't miss that hole. The one on the other side of the ford was twice as bad. . . . Looky yonder! I do believe we're here at last." Zeb pointed down at a motley collection of tents grouped in the inner circle of an ancient fenced-in racetrack.

Lined up near the tents were three airplanes, all painted alike with green markings. A fourth sat some distance away. This last, looking pathetic and forlorn, was only a fuselage on wheels. Several sections of its wings lay in the high grass nearby, while another hung limply from the plane's side as if someone had given up on an attempt to attach it there.

"Lord, have mercy!" Zeb was squinting in the twilight. "I do believe they're trying to put that Jenny's top wing on the bottom!" Zeb gunned the truck down the hill and through the fairgrounds gate. He crossed the track and pulled in alongside the wingless aircraft.

Tommy's eyes, widening with awe and excitement, flew from one airplane to the next. Little shivers rippled along his backbone. They were so beautiful! And at last, *at last* his chance to fly in one was coming!

Zeb's voice seemed to be booming in the quiet left when he killed the truck motor and got out. "Would you look at that, Tom? You and me ain't here a minute too soon. They've even got the prop on backwards. These darn fools prob'ly woulda tried to fly it like that!"

Zeb was walking around the Jenny, mumbling and shaking his head, when a figure hurtled from the nearest tent and began to pound him on the back. "Zeb, you old son of a seahorse! Miz Kelly said you'd be here, but I figured mebbe you'd got some sense in your head and give up on airplanes!"

"I purely wish I'd been born with the brains to do so, Teddy," Zeb answered. "Especially when I find a mess like this waiting for me." Zeb pointed in disgust at the offending wing.

The short, chubby man called Teddy scratched at an almost bald head and placed a hand on his hip. "I tried to tell Yank it didn't look right, but he said that's how the plans showed it."

"Wal then, he must have been standing on his head to read 'em! I never in all my born days . . ."

"Zeb!"

Tommy glanced over his shoulder, looking for the source of the deep, musical voice.

"Miz Kelly! Mighty nice to see you, ma'am." Zeb wiped his big hand quickly on his pants leg before he took her offered one.

Tommy stared. After all Zeb's stories, he'd been sure he knew just what Mrs. Kelly looked like. But this petite, dark-haired young woman bore no resemblance to the muscular Amazon Tommy had pictured. The immaculate condition of her tailored white shirt, jodhpurs, and boots made Tommy keenly aware of how grimy he was.

Mrs. Kelly, however, seemed undisturbed by his appearance when she peered into the truck. "And who's this you brought with you, Zeb?"

"Why, that's my new partner, ma'am. Climb down out of there, Tom, and say 'howdy-do' to Miz Kelly."

Tommy climbed down stiffly, painfully aware that several more people had joined the group around Zeb. He imagined that all of them must be wondering where Zeb could have picked up such a sorry-looking companion.

Zeb, too, seemed to feel that some explanation was needed. "He's little, but he's spunky, folks. And he's about the best natural-born mechanic I ever did see." Zeb paused a second, then turned with dramatic scorn to gesture toward the half-built Jenny. "And it sure looks like mechanics is what you folks need."

A very young man who'd been standing with one foot resting on the Jenny's left wheel, lowered his eyes, flushed in embarrassment, and began to saw back and forth on the ends of the silk scarf around his neck. The others laughed at his confusion, but Mrs. Kelly was still looking at Tommy. "I wonder—is working on airplanes all you want to do, Tom?" she asked.

"No, ma'am," Tommy answered. "That is . . . I mean, I'll be happy to help out with the fixing, but . . ." His eyes drifted toward the dusty fleet around him. ". . . I want to learn to fly them, too," he finished.

Mrs. Kelly's laugh was oddly abrupt. "He's hired," she announced to the group. "At least, I won't have to worry about him drinking on the job. And he's got the flying bug, so I may not even have to pay him." She looked back to Tommy, a cynical smile touching her lips. "How about it, Tom, would you work just for meals and flying lessons?"

Tommy was speechless, but his nod was full of enthusiasm. He was still trying to find words for his gratitude when she murmured, "Pilots—we're all crazy!" Shaking her head, she walked away toward the largest tent.

Chapter

8

TWO MORNINGS LATER NO ONE IN THE CAMP WAS STIR-
ring when the alarm on Yank Minelli's clock went off.
Tommy was aroused at once, then waited through a
teeth-grinding eternity for his host to wake up and
silence the clamor.

Yesterday morning Yank had apologized for the early
awakening. "Y'see, Tom, I'm one of those people who
needs time to wake up. In the Army the other fellas
had to yank me outa bed and drag me along with them
to roll call. I didn't really come to until chow time." The
pilot grinned shyly. "They said they called me 'Yank'
because my real name—Amerigo—made me sound like
a foreigner. But I expect they were thinkin' too about
how they got me out of bed!"

At last the alarm did what it was supposed to do.
Yank rose, groaning, staggered across the tent, and

groped for the clock. It choked off, leaving Tommy in newly appreciated quiet.

Eyes still glazed, Yank began to pull his clothes on. Tommy sighed, got up, and began to dress too. It was no use to wish his tentmate a good morning yet. Yank wanted no conversation until he'd had some coffee.

At first Tommy had felt strange about moving in with Yank. He had wished that the tent Teddy shared with Zeb could have been stretched to hold one more cot. But it had been nice of Yank to offer him shelter, and he certainly hadn't been hard to get to know.

In a lot of ways his new friend reminded Tommy of Mark. Not in looks of course—Yank was tall and skinny with dark brown hair and a prominent nose and Adam's apple. But he was so open—even when he thought he was being subtle—that Tommy found it hard to remember that Yank was actually four years older than he was.

Tommy drifted outside and over to Teddy's tent. All was quiet there. Resigned, he settled onto the grass to wait. He had promised Yank that he would talk with Zeb first thing this morning. Tommy smiled, remembering how Yank had started dropping hints the night before.

"Say, Tom, now that you and Zeb have bought your cots and got your equipment squared away, I suppose you'll be wanting to get right down to work." Yank had nodded along with Tommy. "Yep, that's what I thought. Course you told me that you'd had some practice on the OX-5 motor, but you've never worked on a Jenny, have you?"

Tommy had admitted that this was so. Yank had tried

hard to look as if he'd had a sudden idea. "Say, I just thought of something! Maybe you'd like to help me with my crate—you know, sort of practice on it before you take on Miz Kelly's. Why, with you and Zeb helping, we could probably have it finished in a couple hours." Yank had looked as pleased with himself as a child who's eaten a stolen cookie and doesn't know there are crumbs on his chin.

It had been easy for Tommy to agree to Yank's plan. He knew that Zeb could hardly keep his hands off the half-built Curtiss JN-4. All day yesterday, while they had looked over the work needed on Mrs. Kelly's two ships and scoured the surrounding towns for paint and parts, Zeb had grumbled about Yank's bungled assembly job. Tommy felt certain that Zeb would leap at the chance to remedy Yank's mistakes. He was also certain that, while they were reconstructing the Jenny, its owner would hear a lot more of Zeb's muttering and growling. Tommy suspected that Yank would think it a small price to pay.

While he waited, Tommy's mind kept jumping back to the magic words Mrs. Kelly had spoken on their first day there. *"Pilots—we're all crazy!"* And he felt again the tingle that had gone through him then. It was the first time anyone had called him a pilot. Of course, it wasn't true—yet—but it soon would be. Yank had promised to begin teaching Tommy to fly just as soon as the Jenny was airworthy. The last part of Mrs. Kelly's remark bothered Tommy not at all. She was not the first person to call his interest in flying "crazy."

There were stirrings now from within the tent, and Tommy watched the flap. Teddy Baer's bald head appeared in the canvas doorway. During introductions that first night, Tommy had grinned when he'd heard Teddy's last name. Teddy had made a fist and lightly thumped it on Tommy's thatch of hair. "Okay, you can laugh at my nickname, but, if you want to stay friends with me, don't you ever call me by my real name!"

He had pulled a bedraggled birth certificate from his pocket. "I keep this handy to win bets with." He pointed first to a line that read, "Gwendolyn Elfrida Baer," and then to one further down that said, "Male Caucasion."

Tommy had wondered if this were all a joke, but Teddy had solemnly crossed his heart. "It's the truth, so help me, Tom. Before I was born, my folks promised to name me after my grandmother! I guess you can see why I don't argue about being called 'Teddy'."

This morning Tommy watched "Gwendolyn Elfrida" stretch and yawn several times before his eyes focused.

"Oh . . . morning, Tom. I see Yank's training you to Army hours. Sleep well?"

Without waiting for an answer, Teddy removed the lid from the water bucket resting on a bench by the tent door. He lifted a shallow basin down from its hook, placed it on the bench, and splashed several dippers full of water into it. Wetting a bar of soap, he began to rub lather from its sides as he stared into the small mirror hanging above the bench.

Now other members of the community were stirring. Tommy saw Adrian Villeau emerge from the elegant new sportsman's tent at the end of the line. Zeb had told him that Adrian was Captain Kelly's nephew. "I reckon that's why Miz Kelly feels she has to look after him," Zeb had said in disgusted tones.

61

The darkly handsome Adrian gave a final pat to the careful waves in his sleek hair, then took out the makings and rolled a cigarette with precise, disdainful movements. It dangled, unlit, beneath his pencil line mustache as he strolled across to where Yank was making inept efforts to continue assembling the Jenny.

Tommy felt sorry for Yank, trying to keep working while Adrian watched, a contemptuous smile on his lips. It was the same smile Adrian had used when he'd answered his introduction to Tommy. "Training him to be a mechanic, huh, Zeb? Well, it's okay with me—as long as he doesn't do any learning on *my* ship."

After a moment Adrian ambled on toward where his own aircraft stood slightly apart from the rest. Like his tent, Adrian's airplane was not the typical barnstormer's well-worn Army surplus. It looked as if it had been purchased new from the manufacturer.

Teddy, his cheeks and chin covered with soapy lather, came over and sat down beside Tommy while he waited for his whiskers to soften. They both watched Adrian discover a white splatter of bird droppings on the tail of his Canuck. Teddy chuckled at the look of annoyance that crossed Adrian's face.

"That's what he gets for being in such a hurry last night. With that farmer's daughter waiting for him, he forgot all about putting the tarpaulin over his pretty toy."

Tommy remembered how the others had teased Adrian at supper the night before when one of his young passengers had returned to the field alone in her father's car.

"Why do you think I stay in this business?" Adrian had asked, letting the girl wait while he took a second helping of dessert. "It certainly isn't for the few dollars we can squeeze out of these hicks."

"Listen, Tom." Teddy brought Tommy back to the present by nudging him gently with the handle of his straight-edge razor. "Be on your guard around Adrian today. He'll be looking for a sucker to wash that Canuck for him—and he's good at making promises."

Tommy looked around at Teddy and smiled. "You mean, I should remember rule number one of this business—Always collect your pay before the show?"

Teddy chuckled and slapped Tommy on the back with a damp hand. "Son of a gun! Miz Kelly doesn't need to worry about you. You're more experienced than you look, kid." He stood up and started making tentative strokes down his cheek with the razor as he walked back to the mirror.

"Hey, Tommy boy, how are ya?" Tommy turned to wave at Noah Bauman, who had come out of his tent and was talking to Yank. Noah was dressed like Yank—in leftover army clothes—but there the resemblance ended. Next to Yank's dark curls, Noah's hair looked even whiter, and his face was babyish and sunburned.

As he sauntered on toward Tommy, Noah's friendly grin disappeared and his pale eyebrows shot upward in alarm. "Holy Moses, Tom, don't you know poison ivy when you see it? Get out of that stuff!" Tommy jumped up and was searching the area behind and all around him when Noah broke into laughter. "Gotcha that time. And you, a farmer's son!"

Tommy laughed, too. Noah had given him fair warning during last night's supper. "This is going to be the country's first air circus, Tom, and I'm the clown!"

63

It was Noah who had explained about the air circus. "It's like this—Miz Kelly figures that lots more people will want to try flying if we give 'em their pick of airplanes. They might have had one pilot come barnstorming through. But they've probably never seen *four* planes together—let alone watched them fly in formation. And think of all the stunts we can dream up! Folks will come from miles around once they hear about us."

Yank had gone on. "Yeah, especially when they hear that all this fancy flying and stunts—the whole show— is for free. We'll work fairs and carnivals, maybe some vacation spots—anyplace we can find a crowd."

Tommy had been puzzled. "But, how can you make any money if you give the show for free?"

Adrian Villeau had given a disgusted snort. "There you are, Cynthia, even a kid can see what's wrong with it!"

Mrs. Kelly had turned and half smiled at Adrian, but her voice was cold and measured. "When we charged for our exhibition shows before the war, Adrian, how many people bought tickets?"

Adrian pulled nervously at the small end of his mustache and looked away. "Not many," he admitted.

"Why not?" she demanded.

"Because they could see just about as much of the show by sitting outside the grandstand," Adrian mumbled.

Mrs. Kelly finished in a tone that reminded Tommy of the one Miss Fitzgerald had reserved for students who failed to study the lesson. "Then doesn't it make good sense to advertise a *free* air show before people realize they can see it for nothing anyway?"

Adrian had lapsed into a sullen silence while Teddy explained the rest of the plan to Tommy. "After the show, while folks are all fired up about the wonderful things our airplanes can do, we'll offer to sell rides in those very same airplanes. Why, people will be fighting to give us their money!"

Mrs. Kelly held up a warning finger. "Remember, Teddy, when you talk to the people running the fairs, be sure they understand—we'll put the show on free, but we want the *exclusive* right to sell rides. We don't want any Johnny-come-lately pilots trying to skim off the cream after we have the folks ready."

Adrian spoke again, his voice heavy with discontent. "But I still think whoever takes up the most riders should get the most money. It's only fair!"

Mrs. Kelly snapped back, "I wonder if you'd think so if you owned the oldest airplane instead of the newest and shiniest? I decided that, after expenses were paid, we'd all get an even share of the take—with a double share going to those who do the really dangerous stunts. Anyone who doesn't like that decision doesn't have to stay."

Tommy had watched in admiration as she had stared down her nephew. Clearly, Mrs. Kelly was the boss of the outfit. Zeb had told him that it was Captain Kelly's idea to get exhibition fliers to work together instead of in competition, and Mrs. Kelly was determined to carry on with her husband's plans. But Tommy had not understood until that scene with Adrian last night just how difficult her job must be.

"Well, Zeb, by gosh, you *did* make it out of bed before noon!" Hearing Teddy's teasing, Tommy realized that Zeb had come out of the tent.

"Wal, Tom, what's got you looking so thoughtful this morning?" Zeb accepted the rinsed-out basin from Teddy and began to dip fresh water into it.

Tommy answered slowly, "I was just thinking—Mrs. Kelly has a pretty big job here, running this show."

Zeb splashed the cold water over his face and smoothed his short hair with wet fingers. "That she has, Tom, that she has." He grinned, his eyes lighting up with memories. "But don't you fear—she's up to it. Why, I could tell you some stories..." He stopped as a bell sounded from the mess tent. "But they can wait, son. We'd best hurry on to breakfast now. One of Miz Kelly's most unbreakable rules is, 'If you ain't there when the food's ready, you don't eat!' "

Chapter

9

"C'MON, TOM, LET'S TRY HER OUT!" YANK'S VOICE SHOOK
with eagerness as he and Tommy stood staring at the
completed Jenny. Shortly after sundown the day before,
Zeb, still muttering about all the "dang-fool mistakes"
he'd had to correct, had pronounced the craft airworthy.

Several times that night Tommy had been half awakened by Yank's restless tossing on his cot. This morning
no alarm clock was needed. Dawn had been a mere
suggestion of light when Yank had leaped out of bed
and begun to dress. His excitement had jolted Tommy
awake, and he too had hurried into his clothes.

"Oh, isn't she beautiful, Tom! Isn't she just beautiful!"
Yank had crowed as they stepped outside. Then he had
said, "Let's try her out!" Was he serious?

"Come *on!*" Yank's rough slap on the back got rid
of Tommy's doubts. Pulling on his own leather helmet,

Yank handed another one to Tommy. "Put this on—then climb up in there and fasten your seat belt." He did a strange little shuffle of a dance. "Man, oh man, I can't wait to see how she flies!"

Tommy pulled himself up and onto the reinforced wing section next to the fuselage. Clutching the leather padding, he lowered himself into the front seat and struggled with fastening the belt. Yank continued to issue instructions.

"Hold that stick clear back in your lap, Tom. Don't want her nosing over when the engine starts." He hurried around to stand with his hand on the wooden propeller. "Okay," he yelled. "Switch off?"

Tommy felt his stomach contracting as he tried to remember exactly what Jeff and George had said to each other when starting their plane last summer. "Switch off!" he yelled back, after he found the ignition on his left and made sure it was in the off position.

Yank pulled the propeller full circle several times. Then he stood back and yelled, "Contact!"

Tommy moved a shaking hand to the ignition switch, pushing it to the on position. "Contact!" he answered.

The propeller was horizontal. Yank reached up with both hands and got a firm grip near the tip of one blade. He kicked out with one foot and jerked the propeller around, jumping back as he did so. Several times he repeated these actions—then the engine caught and settled quickly into a steady rumble. Yank jogged a wide circle around the whirling blades and hopped back up onto the wing.

"Okay," he shouted, "let her warm for a few minutes." He remained crouched beside Tommy, impatient as a dog held back from a cat. In moments the pilot leaned far in to push forward the throttle on Tommy's right. "Now, let's run her up."

The engine roared louder, and Tommy watched the four instruments on the panel in front of him jiggle with the vibration. He could feel the wheels straining against the wooden blocks that kept them from rolling. "Good." Yank nodded. "Okay, Tom, throttle her down for a minute."

Tommy eased the throttle back, hoping that he'd adjusted it properly. If he went too far, the engine might die, and Yank would have the hard work of pulling the prop through all over again. Yank nodded a second time and jumped down to pull the chocks away.

As they came free, Tommy gasped. The Jenny was moving—and it had no brakes! The only way to stop it would be to shut down the engine. His hand was moving toward the ignition switch when he felt Yank's weight on the wing. He heard a shout, "Okay, I got her," and the stick he had been clutching to his stomach moved as Yank's hand closed on its counterpart in the rear cockpit. At the same instant the engine roared loud again. They were off, taxiing over the bumpy ground toward the far end of the grass runway.

Tommy was surprised when Yank swung the Jenny around many feet short of the high board fence. The other pilots he had watched had started their takeoff runs as close as possible to that fence.

Watching the throttle in his cockpit move, Tommy felt his heart begin to pound. The plane was beginning its roll down the runway, moving faster and faster. They had gone only a few yards when Tommy felt the tail skid leave the ground and the tail rose until the plane was level. Tommy wanted to shout with joy. Soon they would be in the air!

The roar of the engine was deafening now, but the two occupants still were bounced and jounced as the wheels of the plane refused to lift from the ground. The boy caught a swift glimpse of Zeb and Mrs. Kelly standing in front of Mrs. Kelly's tent. It occurred to Tommy that, when he had stood in that spot watching other takeoffs, the ships had been airborne by that point.

Tommy glanced back at Yank and saw that the pilot's elated look had changed to one of puzzlement as he studied his instruments and the fast-diminishing runway. Suddenly Yank jerked the stick into his lap, and Tommy was slammed hard into his seat as the Jenny rose about twenty feet in the air. The motor seemed to hesitate, and Tommy felt himself lifted against his safety belt as Yank shoved the stick forward to bring the plane's nose back to level. Just below the left wing Tommy saw the tops of rough, gray boards go flashing by and realized that Yank had just managed to clear the fence.

They were climbing now, but too slowly. Peering helplessly through the six-inch windshield, Tommy could see tall trees approaching fast. The Jenny was headed for some large branches that looked suddenly like huge evil fingers held up to swat them from the sky.

At the last moment Tommy felt himself flung to the left. Yank had dropped one wing until its tip pointed almost straight down at the ground. Lying on his side, feeling the reassuring tug of the belt that held him in the seat, Tommy stared ahead at the narrow valley that had miraculously appeared between two mountainous trees.

Yank's last-minute action had turned the Jenny until it had just enough room to scrape through.

As they shot out the other side of the gap, Tommy heard a sharp, "Crack!" and saw a small green branch cling for an instant to one of the struts before it was pulled away by the slipstream. A moment later Yank had leveled out, and the straining engine settled down to a proper roar. Tommy saw that they were directly above the wide creek. Yank was following its gently curving pathway as they climbed—ever so slowly—to a safe altitude.

Again Tommy turned to stare into the back seat. Beads of sweat stood on Yank's forehead, and his face was pale, but he grinned when he felt Tommy's eyes upon him. "Well," he shouted, "I'll bet you're wide awake now!" His eyes fell to the scene below, and he motioned for Tommy to look down.

Tommy obeyed. In a moment he was so entranced by what he saw he forgot how close they had come to crashing. The farmland was laid out like the squares of a checkerboard—brown squares where the fields were newly plowed, pale green squares where early plantings were already yielding the first young sprouts. Except when interrupted by farm ponds and clumps of trees, the lines dividing the fields were amazingly straight and precise.

And the wonderful mixture of smells! Through the crisp morning air, Tommy identified clover and newly cut alfalfa. The odors of hay and grain diluted the tang of manure—producing a sharp, but not unpleasant, aroma. There was even a faint waft of perfume when they passed over a farm wife's flourishing spring garden.

Shifting his gaze to the ship's other side, Tommy saw that they were beginning a lazy circle over the town. With delight he picked out the road that went from the racetrack into the little village. From that he could identify places he had visited in the past few days.

How different the grocery, the hardware store, and the gas station looked from the air! He saw several small boys stepping into the street to wave. Tommy waved back. It was a good feeling to be in the air, instead of one of those who watched from the ground.

Yank shouted something. Tommy turned to see him pointing down at the boys. The nose of the airplane dropped as Yank banked into a dive that aimed them straight for the square in the town's center. Wires in the Jenny's wings screamed as the steep dive brought them down and down, until Tommy thought they would hit the statue of the town's founder. At the last instant Yank leveled off so that they passed several feet above the statue and held that altitude the length of the street.

They zoomed past the boys, so close that Tommy could see their wide eyes and the O's of their mouths as they scurried to safety on the sidewalks. Further down the street, a farmer in a wagon struggled to control his team of horses, his curses rising even above the clatter of the Jenny's engine.

Yank laughed and pulled the Jenny back into a climb. Tommy felt a grand superiority as they rose, free of the small problems that beset the earthbound. He snuggled back into his seat, leaning with the gentle banking turns as Yank spiraled higher and higher. Tommy thought he would burst with sheer pleasure; flying was just as wonderful as he had dreamed it would be.

After a while he felt the plane level off; then Yank was leaning forward to tap his shoulder. "Hey, Tom!" he shouted. "You wanta take her for a while?" Tommy whirled, sure that Yank was teasing, but the pilot held both hands high in the air. "She's all yours!"

For what seemed endless minutes Tommy stared first at Yank's control stick, then at his own. Surely with no strong hands directing either one, the plane would begin to fall. But the Jenny continued in nearly straight and level flight.

Yank shouted again, "She'll fly all day by herself like this. But if we don't want to run out of gas fifty miles from home, we'd better head back toward the track." He reached for the stick and made a graceful turn until they were facing back the way they had come. "Okay, Tom, you got her again," he yelled.

More with gestures than by going through the strain of yelling over the engine noise, Yank showed Tommy how, by pushing the stick to left or right, he could move the ailerons, which were on the outer ends of the upper wings. Tommy was surprised at how far he had to push the stick to one side before the wing on that side dropped. He returned the stick to its original position, and the wing, obedient but without haste, came back to level. A wonderful sense of achievement came over Tommy when, with only a few minutes practice, he was able to rock the wings or hold them level, just as he wished.

Again Yank put his hand on the controls in his cockpit and, with more sign language, demonstrated that the elevators on the tail moved up and down in response to strong pushes forward and back on the stick. Tommy

75

practiced this maneuver—letting the nose of the plane start down, then bringing it back to level, then to climb. He soon learned that the Jenny could not be rushed. Pulling back too sharply for a climb made her protest, but when her pilot kept his controlling movements smooth and patient, she responded in kind.

Tommy practiced intently until he was interrupted by Yank's laughter. "Okay, Tom, you can fly her. Now where you goin' to land her?" Embarrassed, Tommy realized that he had not looked down at the ground since they had turned back. He had no idea where they were. He looked over one side, and then the other, but all the farmhouses and fields looked alike.

"Try the water compass," Yank shouted, pointing forward and a little to the left. Tommy saw a thin curving line glinting silver in the sunlight. As Yank turned the ship toward it, Tommy saw that it was the stream that ran beside the fairgrounds. He searched along its banks. There! He could see the track now, its oval board fence easy to spot once he had the stream as a landmark.

In a moment they were circling for their landing. With a sharp pang of regret Tommy settled back for the end of his first flight. Smoothly the Jenny glided down and came to rest on the bumpy grass strip.

Yank taxied his plane back to its parking space, cutting the engine at exactly the right spot, but Tommy could see that Zeb and Mrs. Kelly, who waited there, were unimpressed by his precision. Zeb reached a gnarled hand to help Tommy down. "You all right, son?" he asked gruffly.

76

"Sure, Zeb," Tommy answered. "It was great!"

"Great, huh?" snorted Zeb. "I don't suppose you know how close you come to havin' your first and last airplane rides all in one package." He turned his full fury toward Yank. "But *you* oughta know. What the devil were you thinkin' of, takin' off short like that?"

Yank's face turned red. "I guess I sort of forgot to allow for old Tom's extra weight." He patted Tommy's shoulder and tried a nonchalant wink. "He doesn't look big enough to make that much difference."

Mrs. Kelly stepped up beside Zeb. Though her voice was controlled, her green eyes blazed with anger.

"And just what is your excuse for buzzing the town? Or haven't you heard me, all the times I've reminded the men? We have to stay in the townsfolk's good graces, or we'll lose the use of this field!"

Yank looked down and scuffed the toe of his army boot in the dust. "I guess I forgot for a minute," he mumbled.

Mrs. Kelly put both hands on her hips and her words were like careful taps of a hammer, driving their point home. "Very well, then, we must make sure your memory doesn't fail you again. First, you will get yourself into town, apologize, and pay for any damage your mischief caused. Second, you are grounded for a week. Third, you will forfeit your share of any money taken in during that week!" She wheeled, started to walk away, then turned back. "One more rule forgotten, Yank, and you are out of the show. Clear?"

Yank nodded, his face betraying his misery. "Clear," he answered.

Zeb stepped closer to shake a warning finger under Yank's nose. "And don't you never offer Tommy no more rides!"

Tommy's heart dropped. He reached for his old friend's sleeve. "But, Zeb . . ." he started to protest.

Zeb shook him off. "No, Tom, don't give me no arguments," he insisted. "Anyone that flies like this fool does is bound to kill hisself, but I'm goin' to make sure he don't take you with him!"

FLYING VERY LOW AND IN GOOD FORMATION, FOUR AIR-
planes thundered by where Tommy sat crosslegged in
front of the bleachers. In spite of his resolve to appear
unimpressed, familiar chills of excitement shivered
through him, and he heard his own voice join the "Ah's!"
that rose from the crowd at his back. No matter that
Tommy had seen this opening number performed in
three towns already, not counting the many rehearsals.
Knowing what was coming only increased the suspense
for him.

As the four planes swooped in, seeming almost to
touch each other, Tommy's mind raced through the
problems involved in this stunt. Would Adrian throttle
back so that the two Jennies flown by Yank and Noah
could stay in tight? Adrian made no secret of his con-
tempt for these slower cousins of his clipped-wing

Canuck. Would that OX-5 engine in the Jenny that Noah flew, the one that Tommy and Zeb had rebuilt last winter, continue to behave itself? Or would it, for some untraceable reason, choose the worst possible time to quit—that time of lowest altitude when Noah would have only moments to choose his crash spot?

And would Teddy, bringing up the rear of the diamond formation in the huge Standard, concentrate so hard on keeping the bulky craft in the air that he would forget to keep its giant propeller a respectful distance from the Jennies' fragile tails?

"That blasted Standard—it's underpowered and over-built!" Zeb had complained to Mrs. Kelly the night before.

"I know, Zeb, I know," she had soothed. "But that's the way the government bought it, so that's the way I had to take it at the surplus sale." She had half turned to include Teddy. "But I think I have some good news for you. Teddy's heard about a Hisso engine that may be available in Haysville, our next stop. How'd you like to put that in the Standard, Zeb?"

Zeb's face had made Tommy want to burst out laughing. Zeb's mouth had twitched into a mere straight line, but his eyes had gleamed, which was as close as he ever came to beaming with pleasure.

Thinking of Zeb, Tommy looked over at the small dressing tent. Zeb would be in there now, getting ready for his part in the show. At first, after their last-minute mechanical checks were finished, Tommy had stayed near Zeb and watched the show from the shade of that tent's awning.

Today, Tommy had decided to move further away—

it was too disturbing to stay closer. Zeb, thinking he was unheard inside the tent, would curse himself softly. "You damned idiot. You ain't got the sense of a flea." And as he struggled into his gleaming white coveralls, he would take furtive sips from a cough syrup bottle, which Tommy had never seen him carry before.

Tommy was still frowning toward the tent when gasps from behind him brought his attention back to the performance. While the crowd watched the three other planes begin a spiraling climb for altitude, Teddy, in the Standard, had slipped away behind a sheltering grove of trees. Working around behind the spectators, he had suddenly swooped over them in a nerve-jangling pass that seemed only inches above their heads.

Instinctively they ducked, then straightened, casting sheepish glances at each other as Teddy flew the Standard away with derisive waggles of its wings. Soon he turned back toward the grandstand, this time aimed toward the open platform from which Mrs. Kelly had introduced the show. She had set aside her megaphone and was holding out a long bamboo pole. From the end of the pole fluttered the largest, brightest handkerchief to be found in the local general store.

Tense silence settled in as the crowd watched the huge Standard bear down upon the slim young woman. At the last possible instant, the airplane veered to one side, a wing tip grazed the pole, and the delighted viewers burst into applause as the Standard sped away with the handkerchief fluttering from the leading edge of its bottom wing.

As Teddy circled back into a landing, Mrs. Kelly picked up the megaphone again and tried to make her voice heard. Most of her speech was drowned out even before it reached Tommy's ears, but her gestures finally lifted the attention of the noisy crowd to the sky. There, high up, Yank and Noah had already begun a mock dog-fight. Within moments, the spectators began taking sides—cheering on the plane they hoped would win.

It was evident that each craft was intent on getting into the best firing position—lined up with the tail of the other. The pilots were using a string of aerobatics, many invented by World War fliers under far more desperate conditions. Although they seemed to be engrossed in their nose dives, snap rolls and spins, the two combatants were bringing their drama nearer as they descended lower and lower.

When the two planes were close enough, the members of the crowd who had taken up for Noah fell into embarrassed silence, for now they could see that a soiled German flag fluttered from his cockpit. For good measure, Noah had donned a German infantryman's helmet —a souvenir that Tommy knew had changed owners through many poker games before coming into Noah's possession.

In contrast, the United States flag attached to Yank's cockpit was spotless, and his helmet was a familiar American one. A moment after that first startled recognition, everyone in the crowd was on his feet and shouting for the destruction of "the dirty Kraut."

Noah played his part well; they could almost see the sneer on his face as he veered and turned. Several times he seemed to have Yank in the sights of his imaginary machine gun. Each time, through obviously superior skill, Yank would avoid disaster, and Noah would sweep past, a victim of his own inept flying. At last Yank pulled into a dramatic and sudden loop, and, before the startled German could blink, the American was coming in behind and slightly above him, with his guns trained on the hated flag. It was certain now that the Kaiser's man was done for. In the next moment a trail of white smoke began to pour from the enemy plane as it twisted helplessly toward the ground.

While the crowd booed the loser, Tommy silently admired Noah's skill. It wasn't easy to hold an open bag of flour into the wind, making that smoke trail, while he guided the Jenny in for a landing.

The members of the crowd gave all their attention to the victor. They waved and cheered as their hero landed and taxied to the grandstand. Yank raised both hands over his head and clasped them in a gesture of victory. Then he climbed over the side of his aircraft, bowed, and in best military posture strode forward to salute Mrs. Kelly.

When the enthusiastic whistles and clapping faded, the onlookers became aware that somewhere a man was shouting, and as one person they turned to look toward the Standard. Tommy grinned. Teddy was right on cue —jumping from his cockpit and running toward Mrs. Kelly and Yank while he pointed wildly toward the heavens. Noah, too, was running toward the platform and motioning skyward. Obediently the spectators tilted their heads back, searching for the cause of the commotion. Directly above the platform, but so high as to be barely visible, they could just make out the fourth airplane, the Canuck piloted by Adrian.

Teddy was holding the megaphone now, reciting his

speech. "He's going to do it, Miz Kelly. He's trying for the record!" Tommy winced a little at the tone of the words. Clearly, Teddy was no actor.

Everyone was staring upward when the Canuck dove, pulled up and over onto its back, then dove again, beginning a series of loops. Teddy, Noah, and Yank loudly counted each one and the audience soon joined in. There was tension in their chant as they saw that each loop was bringing Adrian closer to the ground. Only Tommy noticed when Mrs. Kelly slipped away toward where Noah had parked her Jenny.

The spellbinding count reached thirty-nine before Adrian finally gave up his flirtation with death and leveled out to land. Tommy imagined he could hear Mrs. Kelly's sigh of relief. He knew that the number of loops agreed upon had been thirty.

As Adrian's wheels touched down on the landing strip, an engine roared from the far end of the field, and the forgotten "German" airplane taxied toward the grandstand. Mrs. Kelly was operating the controls, and in the front cockpit she carried a passenger—Zeb. To Tommy, Zeb looked far younger, almost a stranger, with his gray hair concealed by a white helmet that matched his coveralls.

As soon as Mrs. Kelly's Jenny had cleared the runway, Tommy ran forward to help Yank and Teddy pull a canvas tarpaulin out onto the field. On it was heaped a sizable pile of hay. For a while the excited onlookers speculated about what was to happen. They watched intently, but the Jenny seemed to be heading away from the field.

"Come on, Sarah," a man mumbled in disappointment.

"I guess that's all. We'll go now and see if your pickles won that prize." A few others began to drift away, but a shout from the remaining spectators brought them hurrying back. The Jenny had turned around at last, and, as it clattered closer, the far-sighted members of the crowd were finding it hard to believe their own eyes.

There were still two people with the ship, but Zeb was no longer in the front cockpit. He now stood in the center of the top wing, his legs spread wide apart, his hands braced arrogantly on his hips!

When Mrs. Kelly made a pass in front of the gaping spectators, a fat man behind Tommy sneered. "Ah, he ties himself down—that's how he does it!" As if to prove this a lie, Zeb suddenly bent forward, resting the top of his helmet and both hands on the wing. A moment later his feet were kicking into the air, and he straightened into a headstand. He held that position for a full circuit of the field. Then he righted himself and began to work his way down onto the lower wing.

Tommy could see the sleeves and pants legs of Zeb's white coveralls whipping in the slipstream as he inched along, clinging to struts and reinforcing wires. While Mrs. Kelly maneuvered back and forth, skillfully keeping Zeb in view of the audience, he worked his way out to the tip of a lower wing. He was directly in front of the grandstand when he swung down to hang by his hands from the skid underneath the wing. The crowd's cries increased to cheers and loud applause.

After a few minutes Zeb thrust with his legs to pull himself back onto the wing. Unexpectedly one of his hands slipped. There was a collective catching of breath —then the spectators chuckled at what they thought had been a deliberately faked blunder. But Tommy was puzzled. Zeb had never used that slip in the act before.

Now Zeb was up, crouched on the lower wing, and slowly moving in toward the fuselage. A few careful steps farther and he was in position to clamber down onto the axle bar of the undercarriage. When he reached that point, between the plane's two wheels, he seemed to hesitate for a long time. At last he gripped the axle with his hands and dropped down to dangle below the ship, facing the tail. Another sudden twist and Zeb's legs were up and over the bar. One more pause, then his hands came free and he fell back, hanging upside down and facing forward, held only by his knees locked around the axle bar.

The people behind Tommy were sitting far forward in their seats. Tommy looked at the intense excitement on their faces—and wondered. For him, the skillful aerobatic flying was the high point of the show, but the crowds always seemed to like this crazy stunt the best. Maybe what the oldtimers muttered was true. Maybe people really did come to an air show with the secret hope that they would see someone killed. But he didn't want to believe that.

He turned to watch Mrs. Kelly swing out wide, preparing for the final, low sweep past the grandstand. She was trying to slow the Jenny as much as possible without risking a stall—and at the same time to line up to fly directly over the pile of hay. Closer they came, closer, and Tommy could see Zeb inching free of the bar until he seemed to hang by his heels as he strained to watch his approaching target.

The Jenny was directly above the haystack now, and

Zeb was dropping—but not quite onto its center. He hit in the shallower hay at the far side and bounced on down onto the hard-packed dirt of the runway. Then he was rolling over and over as Tommy, Yank, and Noah raced to his side.

Chapter

11

BEFORE THEY COULD LIFT HIM, ZEB SAT UP. HIS FACE was scratched and bloody and ingrained with particles of dirt, but he managed to wave at the spectators. They roared back in approval. Zeb turned away from them and winced as he tried to stand. With reluctance he accepted the support of Yank and Noah on either side. "Git me the hell out of here, fellas," he grunted. "I'm a goldurn hero now, and I don't think nothin's broke, but I'll sure be a black-and-blue wonder tomorrow."

There was relief in Teddy's voice as he began the closing speech of the show. "Ladies and gentlemen, we thank you for your kind attention. We have shown you the many wonders of flying. But why not experience this thrill for yourselves? Buy a ticket for only five dollars, and any one of our daring pilots will take you aloft in the aircraft of your choice."

Ignoring his words, the people were beginning to move out of the stands. Teddy's recitation faded as he realized that Zeb's accident had been too-convincing proof that flying could be dangerous as well as thrilling. He began to stammer unrehearsed, disastrous phrases. "Take a chance, folks . . . Hardly ever happens . . . Not much danger . . ." The members of the crowd speeded up their movement toward the exits.

Suddenly a commanding voice boomed out over their heads. "STOP!" Tommy turned with the others to stare at a stocky, ruddy-faced man in a large-checked suit who had snatched the megaphone from Teddy's hands. "What's the matter with you people? Didn't you hear what this man said? He's offering you the chance of a lifetime! Why, do you realize who that flier *is?*"

The new announcer flung a dramatic, pointing gesture at Adrian, who was startled into jerking upright from his graceful slouch against the Canuck. "Have you ever in your whole life—*will* you ever in your whole life have an opportunity like this? To fly with a *genuine war hero,* our own Captain Winslow, that's something you can tell your grandchildren about!" The stranger's voice dropped to an intimate, humorous tone. "After all, ladies and gentlemen, the only person in trouble here today was a man who wanted to leave the airplane before it landed! I don't think any of *you* would try that!"

The listeners snickered and pushed forward, drawn toward the speaker—who suddenly pushed back his straw hat and cupped an ear toward someone in the front row. "What's that you say, friend? You've already had a ride in an airplane? My dear fellow! I shrink from making comparisons, but that's like turning down a ride in a Pierce Arrow because you've already ridden in a Ford truck!"

The listeners laughed again, more at ease now. The stranger waved a puffy hand toward Adrian's plane. "Why this luxurious craft is *brand new*, my friends, with every feature for your comfort and safety. So, just line up—line up, now, and have your five dollars ready!"

The man swung around to hiss at a dumbfounded Teddy, "Quick, get out there and collect their money before they have a chance to change their minds!" Teddy, tickets in hand, stumbled forward while persuasive words once more issued from the megaphone. "Don't push, don't shove, my good people! Captain Winslow is as honest as he is handsome. I promise you, as sure as my name is Rutherford B. Parker, that he'll make certain every single one of you gets to fly. I *guarantee* you'll always remember this day with pride—the day *you* became a part of the wonderful new Air Age!"

It was after dark when the troupe gathered in the mess tent to divide the day's receipts. Mrs. Kelly entered last, accompanied by Rutherford Parker.

"Well, boys," Mrs. Kelly announced, "our take today was bigger than ever before. I guess we have to admit that Mr. Parker here did us a favor ... though I'm not sure I endorse his methods."

"Yeah," muttered Yank. "Where was that wonderful war hero, Captain Winslow? Looked like old 'Bad-back-kept-me-out-of-the-Army' Villeau to me."

Adrian bolted up from his sprawled pose. "What are *you* griping about? I'm the one who had to hop all the yokels! If it weren't for me, there wouldn't be anything to divide up tonight."

Noah threw him a mocking grin. "My goodness, Captain Winslow, wouldn't the Canadians be surprised to hear that their little military trainer is really a 'modern luxury aircraft'!"

Before Adrian could retort, Mrs. Kelly interrupted. "The fact remains, boys, that Mr. Parker does have a fine voice for announcing. . . . The point is—he's asked me if I'll take him on to do that job for us steady. What do you think?"

There was a long silence. Teddy broke it, his voice more definite than his usual easygoing drawl. "I say yes. You and me know flying, Miz Kelly, but we aren't much on talking to an audience. That's been the big weakness in our show all along."

Mrs. Kelly glanced around. "You all see it that way?" One by one the others nodded. "Very well, Mr. Parker." She addressed him directly for the first time. "We'll try you out for a while. But I want to make one thing clear. This has always been a reasonably honest show, and I mean to keep it that way."

Parker smiled. "Of course, Ma'am," he agreed. "You're the boss!" But his eyes never quite met hers.

Zeb's voice broke in from the cot in the corner where they had tried to make him comfortable. "That ain't all our problems, you know. We have to find a new stunt man. Even if I wasn't all stove up, it's time I quit. I got to admit it—I'm too old."

Tommy spoke before he knew that he meant to. "But *I'm* not!" he said.

The others stared at him. "Are you crazy, Tom?" Zeb shouted. "Wingwalking's no kid's game!"

"And Tommy's no kid, Zeb," Mrs. Kelly murmured. Zeb, taken by surprise, was silent.

Finally Mrs. Kelly said, "You two will have to settle this between you. In the meantime I'll handle the stunts." She went on briskly. "Tomorrow we move on to Haysville. That's where that Hisso engine is, Zeb. I'd like Tommy to drive you out to look at it, if you feel up to it."

Tommy was sure Zeb would go on protesting the next day. But, beyond asking directions, he scarcely spoke until they stood in a cornfield, gazing at a badly-wounded Jenny. The farmer who owned the wreck announced that he was only too glad to sell its Hispano-Suiza engine. "Darn near killed myself in that thing." He kicked at a detached, crumpled wing. "It can lay there and rot for all I care!"

Tommy caught his breath. All his life he had dreamed of owning an airplane. "Would you sell the Jenny, sir?" he asked eagerly.

"*Sell* it?" The owner uttered a bitter laugh. "I'll *give* that pile of junk to anyone who'll haul it away!"

"Now, Tom," Zeb warned. "I know what you're thinkin', but that thing ain't even fit for spare parts. You couldn't rebuild it."

While Zeb turned back to complete his deal with the farmer, Tommy's chin came up. I couldn't, huh? he thought. You might just be mistaken about *that*, Zeb.

On the way back to the circus, Zeb was still silent, and Tommy's mind was free to plan. So far, his earnings from the show had been just food and a place to sleep. But anyone who did stunts got a double share of the day's receipts. "If I started getting that much," Tommy thought, "I could salvage that wreck in no time. Zeb just has to teach me . . ."

"Wal, Tommy," Zeb spoke suddenly. "You still think you want to learn wingwalking?"

Startled at how Zeb's thinking had followed his own, Tommy nodded.

"I guess I got no right to stand in your way," the old man grumbled. "But I been thinkin'—there might be some gadgets I could make for you. It ain't never a *safe* job, but mebbe I can give you a little insurance."

A month later, Tommy stood in the dressing tent, adjusting one of the "insurance" features Zeb had designed —a body harness that could be clipped to safety wires on the airplane. He'd been tempted not to bother with the thing—Zeb was really getting like Ma with his worrying—but it was easier to wear it than to argue. As he pulled his white coveralls over the harness and fastened them up, his thoughts went to the stunt that he, Teddy, and Mrs. Kelly were adding to the act today. "Lotta good this contraption will do me there," he muttered. He paced to the doorway and back, full of the restless excitement he felt before each performance. "Poor Zeb," Tommy thought, remembering how quiet his friend had been after watching their practice this morning. "Bet he was trying to figure how to rig a safety net!"

Parker's bellow resounded into the tent. ". . . Champion of All Stunt Men!" Tommy, reaching up to cinch the strap on his white helmet, ran out and hopped onto the wing of the Standard. Teddy was already in position in the rear cockpit, and Zeb stood waiting to pull through the prop on the new Hisso. Glancing at the motor that he had helped to install, Tommy paused, thinking of the disabled Jenny from which it had been removed. He felt a warm flood of pleasure, remembering how fast his savings were growing.

"Tommy, this ain't no place to be daydreamin'." Zeb was staring up at him. "You okay?"

Tommy grinned. "I'm fine, Zeb. What are you worried about? With all these extra wires and belts you fixed up for me, I'm as safe as a baby in its mother's arms." He swung into the front cockpit, stood erect, and gave the thumbs up signal to Teddy.

Minutes later the Standard was taxiing toward the grandstand. The long white scarf around Tommy's neck began to ripple behind him in the blast from the slipstream. He braced himself to stand solid, remembering to smile and wave as he passed in front of the audience.

As soon as the plane lifted from the ground, Tommy pulled himself out of the cockpit. The wind was ferocious, tugging locks of hair from under the white helmet and flattening the coveralls against his body. Holding with all his strength to the extra supports, he mounted the top wing and positioned himself in its center.

Just before the Standard turned back toward the grandstand, he remembered to snap his body harness to the waiting safety wires. He stood erect, thrust his feet wide apart, and placed his hands on his hips.

Tommy supposed the crowd below was applauding, or shouting with approval, as he upended into the headstand. But he could hear nothing above the roar of the wind, the whistling of the wires, and the clanking drone of the Hisso.

With blood rushing into his face, Tommy waited until the Standard had circled the field. Then he lowered his feet and straightened, looking for a good hold on the closest strut. He was glad it was time to release the safety wire. He liked it better when he was protected only by his own strength and balance.

His movements were confident as he inched down onto the lower wing and began a careful progress toward its distant tip. The excitement he'd felt before the show mounted. He wasn't afraid of these forces that tried to break his hold. He knew what he was doing. If anyone below was hoping to see a fall, Tommy wasn't about to oblige.

Near the tip he knelt, reaching under to grasp the wing skid. He was already swinging down to hang by his hands when he saw the safety wires Zeb had placed here. "Oh well," he answered a twinge of guilt. "I'll re-member to hook up next time."

After a few minutes of hanging below the skid, Tommy pretended that one hand had lost its grip and let himself dangle by the other. Jerking and twisting in an imitation of fear, he glanced down, hoping that his pretence was as realistic as Zeb's actual slip had been. He laughed, the sound swallowed by the surrounding noises. This wasn't such a bad job—at least until he got a chance to be flying. And the more he performed, the more he'd earn, and the closer he'd be to getting that wreck.

At last Tommy moved in next to the fuselage. He gave Teddy a wide smile, and kept going, climbing down onto the spreader bar between the landing wheels. This was the point where Zeb's act had been changed. No longer would Tommy drop into a pile of hay. Parker said that was old stuff.

Tommy reached down and began to untie several knots on strings that secured a coil of fat rope. When the ties fell away, the slipstream pulled the heavy strand out to its full length. From the point where it was attached to the axle, the rope had been knotted about every twenty inches.

Tommy glanced down. As in their rehearsals, Mrs. Kelly's timing was perfect. Her Jenny was well off the runway and climbing to where he and Teddy circled in the Standard. Tommy grasped the rope with both hands and wrapped his legs around it. He began a slow descent. There was no time now for dreams of rebuilding an airplane. Every effort must be concentrated on perfect timing.

Mrs. Kelly, in the Jenny's front cockpit, maneuvered up and under the Standard, avoiding the end of the rope, which blew toward her propeller's flashing edges. The two planes turned together, back toward the grandstand. Now Teddy and Mrs. Kelly had their speeds exactly even, and Mrs. Kelly was keeping the empty rear seat of her Jenny tight in under the Standard's wheels. As quickly as he could, Tommy went hand-over-hand down the remainder of the rope until his legs hung free.

The Jenny rose to meet him, its rear seat coming close, closer. He was above it, the toe of his sneaker touching the cowling. He hesitated. Now seemed to be the right moment. With one hand he let go. In that instant the Jenny hit a small air gust and bounced away.

Surprised, Tommy felt a real twinge of the panic that he had faked earlier in the act. It *hurt*, this sudden cramping of his stomach muscles, and it did not entirely go away even after both hands were back on the line. Swallowing hard, he felt again with his feet while he tried to look straight down. There, the cockpit was placed exactly right. He released his hold on the last knot and dropped into the empty seat.

As soon as Teddy felt the loss of weight, he swung the Standard out and away. Mrs. Kelly banked around for one last triumphant sweep in front of the grandstand. Tommy stood up and waved to the crowd. He wore the smile that Parker insisted upon, but it did not stop a slight trembling in his knees. If he had let go that first time . . . too early . . .

Suddenly a picture of his mother's face flashed through his mind. In her eyes were the fear and worry of the day that they had waited in the doctor's office for word about Mark. For the first time Tommy realized that his parents might be suffering a similar anxiety about him.

A moment ago he had brushed as close to death as Mark once had done, and strangely, he had the notion that his family knew it. "But that's ridiculous," he thought. "They don't even know where I am."

Chapter
12

THE NEXT DAY, SITTING CROSS-LEGGED IN THE SHADE FROM the Standard's lower wing, Tommy tried to keep the sun's glare off the writing tablet in his lap. He scratched at his right eyebrow with the end of a pencil as he read over what he had written:

Dear Ma, Pap, and Mark,

I am fine and hope you are the same. I'm sorry I didn't write before this, but I have been awful busy. Zeb let me come down here with him. Now we are both working for Mrs. Kelly's Air Circus.

It's a real good show, and they treat me fine. Mrs. Kelly is teaching me to fly some. She says I'll soon be ready to solo.

I wish I could see all of you. I hope you aren't mad at me for leaving, but I just had to. Someday I'll have my own airplane, and I'll give you rides.

I know you'll really like flying once you try it.

Please don't worry about me.

Love,

Tommy

He smiled down at the line, "Mrs. Kelly is teaching me to fly." Several times at the end of their stunt practice she had taken him up in her Jenny and let him handle the controls. Yesterday she had let him land it. And, in a moment of unexpected praise, she had told Tommy that he was a natural pilot.

Remembering her words, he decided that his promise to bring home his own plane didn't seem as foolish as Pap would think it. "After all," Tommy thought, "I'm saving up money pretty fast, and, last I heard, that Jenny was still back in Haysville."

As he sealed and addressed the letter, his ears caught the faint clatter of an approaching plane. Tommy frowned toward the noise. Several times other barnstormers had seen the Kelly Circus's advertising and tried to sneak in and steal customers by undercutting the price of a ride. It was usually a difficult task for Mrs. Kelly to make the fairground officials stick by their exclusive contract. Tommy hoped this plane didn't mean more trouble.

As the aircraft came on, Tommy had a feeling that there was something familiar about it. It's unique paint job was now clearly visible—red and silver stripes fanning out over the two sets of wings. Of course! Even before he could see the large black letters on the side, he knew that, turned right side up, they would spell JEFF JOHNSON.

In another few minutes the plane was circling in for a landing. Soon it taxied over and swung into place beside the Kelly fleet. George Letic, as sloppily dressed as ever, was the first to alight. He had a set of chocks braced against the ship's wheels before Jeff lowered himself to the ground. Except that his limp was scarcely noticeable, Jeff had not changed either. In his immaculate jacket and breeches, with puttees wrapped around the calves of his legs, he gave Tommy and the others who watched the feeling that they were about to be inspected by royalty.

"You there," Jeff called, pointing with his leather glove at a perplexed-looking Yank. "Who's in charge here?"

"Uh, Mrs. Kelly, s—" Yank had frozen into military attention. Tommy was amused at the way he had barely stopped himself from calling the new arrival "sir." It was as if Yank felt he ought to salute, but just couldn't place this very important stranger.

"And where might I find the *lady?*" Jeff asked, his voice making the last word questionable. Tommy stiffened. He didn't like anyone using a tone of sarcasm when speaking of Mrs. Kelly.

Neither did Yank. "Mrs. Kelly is in her office," he replied coldly. "She's too busy to see visitors." He turned his back in obvious dismissal.

Tommy hurried forward. "George! George Letic!" he called. George turned, the look on his face saying plainly that he was not used to being noticed when Jeff was center stage. Tommy held out his hand. "Do you remember me—Tommy Davison?"

George narrowed his gray eyes and studied Tommy, then said, "Of course! You're the young fella worked so hard for us one day when we was stormin' around Pittsburgh last summer."

Jeff's face had shown no recognition, only a flash of annoyance at the way he was being ignored. A few seconds later, however, his expression changed. He stepped over to offer his hand to Tommy. "Why yes...uh... Tommy, wasn't it? Good to see you again. Are you with the Kelly outfit?"

"Yes, I am," Tommy answered, quickly releasing Jeff's soft, damp palm. He turned to George. "I'm a mechanic and wingwalker now, but before long, I'll be a pilot."

"Well, listen to you!" George shook his head. "I guess when we give a kid airplane fever, we don't make it a light case. How long—"

"Tommy," Jeff interrupted, "I'd like to see your boss. Would you ask the lady if I could have a few minutes of her time?"

"Nope." Tommy smiled, but sent a challenging glance straight into Jeff's eyes. "Not unless you pay me what you owe me."

"What I owe you!"

George burst into laughter and gave his partner a hearty slap on the back. "Ha, your sins are catching up with you, Jeff. This is one of them kids you promised rides to and then sneaked off before they got them." George glanced back to Tommy. "Look, Tom, what we're here for is to ask about joining up with you folks. How about if I give you that ride whilst Jeff has a chat with your boss?"

A half hour later, Mrs. Kelly was letting Jeff into the office tent just as Tommy and George circled the field and headed east, following the line of the railroad tracks. "You want to fly her?" George shouted.

"You bet!" Tommy answered. Eagerly he took the stick and began to review the lessons Mrs. Kelly had given. Pull back on the stick and bring the nose up until the Jenny was almost stalled. Then push the stick forward to recover. Push the stick to the right and use light rudder to bank into a right turn, then use opposite pressure and rudder to level the ship. Now a bank to the left . . .

It seemed only minutes until George interrupted the precious practice time. "Hey, Tom, we been gone a long time. Better be getting back. Can you find the way?"

Tommy nodded. He knew enough now never to lose his points of reference on the ground. One more bank to the right while his eyes located the rails below—and he followed them westward until they were over the fairground.

On the ground, as they climbed out of their cockpits, George said, "You're a fine pilot—no doubt of that. But, golly Moses, Tom, don't ever give a ride like that to a paying passenger!" Tommy halted, staring at George in puzzlement. "I ain't been sick in an airplane for a *long* time," George declared, rolling his eyes comically. "But I do believe five more minutes of that rockin' from side to side and up and down woulda done it!"

George gave Tommy a good-natured pat on the shoulder as they began to walk toward the office tent. "Next time you want to practice, you go ahead up by yourself. Anybody who's learned to do all that and not lose sight of the iron compass, don't need *my* help."

Cynthia Kelly and Jeff were walking toward them.

Mrs. Kelly said, "Tommy learns quickly and works well —even when the job is not the one he'd like best." She laid her hand lightly on Tommy's arm. "That's how he got where he is with this show." She gazed meaningfully at the two men. "Anyone who works for me has to be willing to help where he's needed."

"Sounds fair to me, ma'am," George drawled. Jeff had lost his princely manner during the interview. He nodded soberly.

Mrs. Kelly went on, "Well, Tom, looks like you'll have some relief on stunt work. Jeff here says he and George can do just about anything in that department." She was turned slightly away from George and did not see the astounded look he threw toward Jeff. She continued speaking to Tommy. "And since you're an experienced mechanic now, you'll still get one share of the take on days when you don't do stunts."

Her voice was all business as she addressed the two pilots. "You two can pitch your tent at the end of the line there. Don't be long about it—dinner will be ready soon."

The mention of food sent Jeff and George into instant action. They hurried to unload their meager gear and began to set up camp just beyond Adrian's tent. Mrs. Kelly, her eyes still on the newcomers, said, "Well, Tom, what do you think? I'm happy to get an extra plane for the show, but I'm not so sure about adding new men."

She didn't seem to expect an answer—it was more as if she were murmuring to herself. They saw Adrian emerge from his quarters, engrossed in conversation with the show's new announcer. Mrs. Kelly's voice took on a rare, discouraged tone. "I used to trust my instincts, but

I'm afraid they've led me wrong several times." She was frowning at her nephew and Parker.

After a long moment, Mrs. Kelly's attention returned. "Did you get that letter to your family finished, Tom? I'm going into town first thing in the morning. I could mail it for you."

"Oh, yes ma'am!" Tommy blushed, remembering that he had not returned what he had borrowed. "I left your writing paper with my things. I'll run and get it for you."

"No rush." Mrs. Kelly sat down on the bench in front of her tent and motioned toward the place beside her. "I have a minute before I have to check on things in the mess tent. Sit down and talk with me." Tommy, surprised, sat on the edge of the rough wooden seat.

Mrs. Kelly smiled over at him. "Do you come from a big family, Tom?" It was the first time he had ever heard her ask a personal question.

"No, ma'am," Tommy replied. "There's just Mark— my younger brother—and Ma and Pap."

Mrs. Kelly's voice softened. "Do you miss them?"

Tommy answered truthfully, "Well, at first I didn't. Everything here was so new and different—I guess I hardly thought about them. And I had so much to learn . . . about the planes . . . and all . . ."

There was a teasing lilt in Mrs. Kelly's tone. "You say 'planes' the way other people say 'diamonds.' Still crazy about them, aren't you?"

Tommy gave her a shy grin. "Yes, ma'am."

"But you'd rather be the one flying the airplane than out there climbing all over it, right?"

"Yes, *ma'am!*" Tommy had startled himself with the

104

vehemence of his answer. He hurried into a correction. "But I can *do* it, if that's what we have to do."

" 'What we have to do,' " Mrs. Kelly echoed, her expression faraway. "What strange things we've gotten ourselves into with that reason! To draw the crowd—to bring the paying customers—we've 'had to do' crazier and crazier stunts, to act like circus clowns, or like maniacs bent on suicide! ... Sometimes I wonder if we haven't missed our whole purpose, Tom. I wonder what Mike would think if he could see what's become of his show."

Tommy was anxious to defend her. "Why, he'd be proud of you! Not many people would even have tried to carry on his plans. And we had to keep up with what others were doing."

"Oh, we've done that—and topped them! We've led the parade." Her lips twisted with irony. "Wouldn't it be a joke if we find out we've led everyone the wrong way!" She leaned back and shrugged her shoulders. "So —you say you didn't miss your folks at first. And now?"

Tommy's answer was cautious. "Well, yesterday ... I just felt ... it was wrong not to tell them where I was. They're probably worrying. Even if we did argue, they care about me."

Mrs. Kelly's look combined surprise and awe. "How wise you are! If only *I* had realized that sooner ..."

"You!"

"I ran away, too, Tom." She stared down at her trim boots. "My parents told me Mike was a fool. Said no one could make a living from these crazy flying machines." Mrs. Kelly glanced over at the nearby planes, her face a mixture of defiance and sadness as she relived that long-ago quarrel. "When I learned to fly—and married Mike!—they said I'd disgraced them. Told me I wasn't their daughter anymore. I was so hurt—so *angry* —I swore I'd never speak to them again."

"But you got over it?" Tommy wasn't sure what she wanted of him. "Didn't you?"

"Not in time." She shook her head slowly. "After about a year, my mother wrote to us. I was too proud to answer. I never even told them when Mike was killed."

Tommy was too stunned to comment. He could only wait in uncomfortable silence until she continued.

"Then one day, I got another letter—from their lawyer. My parents had died in the flu epidemic. What little they had they'd left to Mike and me."

"So they were sorry."

"Oh, yes, and *they* tried to say so." She turned tragic eyes to his. "Oh, Tom, you never want to know what that's like—to be so *terribly* sorry—when its too late!" The eyes showed a glint of tears before she turned her head away. In a moment she stood up. "I'd better get on over to check on dinner."

They began to stroll toward the mess tent. "So now," she continued, "I just try to keep this show running. I'm always hoping it will turn out the way Mike thought. People will ride in our planes and realize . . . realize that airplanes can change the world!"

Tommy's reaction was instant. "And they will!"

"Yes, *you* know it." There was a tinge of doubt in her agreement, but she smiled. "You're so like Mike! No one had to sell either of you on aviation's possibilities. You both knew from the first time you saw an airplane." She shook her head. "If only we could give some of these government people your foresight."

She stopped at the flap of the cook tent and glanced back. "And if only we didn't have so many people around who see airplanes as toys. Or as a new front for an old con game!" Once more she was staring across the field at Adrian and Parker.

Chapter

13

AS HE DRAINED THE LAST TRICKLE OF GASOLINE FROM THE Canuck and carried the full can away to the supplies tent, Tommy wondered why he had let Adrian talk him into doing this. Adrian had said it was just a joke—and he'd paid Tommy in advance. But much as Tommy liked earning extra money, he couldn't forget what Mrs. Kelly had said just last week about con games.

"Well," Tommy thought, "if I'm mixed up in one, it's too late to back out now." Just as he set the can down, a rusted black car came out of the twilight. It turned off the road and screeched to a stop next to the Canuck. Adrian and Parker jumped out, followed by two middle-aged townsmen. The strangers were almost identical, even to the matching unsteadiness of their steps.

Tommy, watching and listening from the tent entrance, fingered the money Adrian had paid him. He hoped he wouldn't be sorry that he'd taken it after he found what Adrian was up to.

"I'd like to thank you again for that feast, Harold," Parker was saying as he patted the shorter of the men on his thin shoulders. "The steak was excellent."

"Nothing's too good for good friends," Harold replied. "Right, Gerald?"

"Right!" Gerald brayed. "And now our good friends are going to take us for a free ride, ain'tcha, friends?"

"Sh-h-h." Adrian held up a warning finger and glanced around. "We're bending the boss lady's rules, you know. But after all, if a fella can't give away a ride now and then, what's the use of owning an airplane?"

"What's the use!" echoed Gerald and Harold, exchanging triumphant glances. Tommy remembered that he had seen the two before. Several times they had watched the air circus performances but had never seemed willing to buy a ticket afterward.

" 'Course you'll have to just top off my gas tank, you understand," Adrian purred. "Don't want to risk running out of gas up there, do we?"

"No, sir-ee." The brothers shook their heads. "We got the gas just like you said." Harold lifted a large can from the back floor of the car and handed it to Gerald. Gerald passed it on to Parker who lifted it to Adrian, now on a ladder.

Adrian poured the whole can into the fuel tank. "More," he called down. The bucket brigade transferred a second can from the car to the airplane. "Well, that didn't quite fill it, but it ought to be enough," Adrian declared. "Okay, boys, who's first?"

The brothers answered together, then Gerald drew

himself up with dignity. "I am older by five minutes—I shall go first."

Harold's face reddened. "I'm sick of that dumb old excuse!" he yelled.

"Tut, tut. There's a simple solution," Parker injected. "Why not accompany each other? Certainly the two of you together couldn't weigh as much as some of the ladies we've taken up." His hands spread wide to indicate the ample proportions of those earlier passengers.

The suggestion met with instant approval from the twins. Though they ended up wedged so tightly into the forward seat that they had to make any movement by mutual agreement, they seemed content. Parker pulled the prop through, Adrian gave throttle to the plane, and away it went, using every inch of the runway to get enough lift for the triple load.

Tommy strode out to where Parker stood watching. "What was that all about?" he asked.

Parker's face took on mocking dismay. "Why, poor Adrian and I have just had ourselves bamboozled by a couple of sharpsters. Those locals were just too shrewd to pay for a ride. They finagled us into giving them a free one!"

Tommy snorted. "Free! What about the cost of those two cans of gasoline?"

Parker's short, sharp laugh reminded Tommy of the yip of a fox. "To say nothing of the cost of two steak dinners with all the trimmings! Let me tell you, Tommy my boy, those two horsetraders spare no expense to set up a deal. Why, I imagine we could have wangled three cans of gas out of them—if you could have kept on siphoning it off somehow."

"Sounds to me like they already paid a lot more for their ride than the regular customers do."

"Ah, now wait a minute, son." Parker held up a hand. "Don't be so fast to judge. They got exactly what they were after—a free ride. And they'll brag about that to their friends for many a month." He snickered. "Of course, they won't bother to remember about the dinners or the gas. They're determined to believe they got something for nothing."

Tommy heard the Canuck returning. "Didn't give them much of a ride," he said.

Parker winked. "With as much booze as they had in them, all Adrian had to do was keep waggling the wings a little. They probably begged him to bring them down."

Sure enough, when the Canuck rolled to a stop, the two passengers fought each other to be the first back on solid ground. When they finally cooperated enough to unwedge themselves, they hastened to the shelter of some nearby trees. Tommy, listening to their pathetic, gagging moans, was repelled by the smirks on the faces of Adrian and Parker.

"Well, there's two that will never fly again," Tommy snapped. "Scare half of them and make the rest sick, and pretty soon we'll be fresh out of customers. Really smart!"

"Now, just a minute, my big-mouthed friend!" Parker stepped forward menacingly. "Are you implying that we're stupid?"

"I think that's an appropriate word." Cynthia Kelly's cold voice came from the shadows. "Dishonest and conniving are two other good ones." She stepped out to face Parker. "I suggest that you and Adrian help your new friends get cleaned up and then see them safely home. Maybe the walk back from town will help you remember what I said about keeping this show honest."

Tommy's face burned as he reached into his pocket for the money Adrian had paid him. "I guess I was in on it too, Mrs. Kelly. Adrian gave me this to drain his gas tank, but I didn't know what he was going to do."

"Keep it this time, Tom. But next time, remember—it's a good idea to know exactly what you're getting paid for." She whirled to confront her nephew. "Seems to me we told *you* that, Adrian, the time your uncle found out you were flying smugglers across the border. I thought you'd learned something then, or I'd never have let you come back with the show."

"Oh, come on, Cynthia. This was just a joke. They were begging for it!"

"Any more jokes like this, and you'll no longer be with us. That goes for you too, Parker I don't even know why I'm giving either of you a second chance." She glanced at the two green-faced passengers who were stumbling back from the clump of trees. "Maybe because my father used to say, 'A man can be cheated only by himself.' "

A few nights later Tommy sat watching Zeb while the old man fitted a new safety harness on George. Mrs. Kelly's lecture was still strong in Tommy's mind. Suddenly, as though his thoughts had been put into action, a furious shout rang out, ". . . cheating!" The word had exploded from the next tent where Jeff, Adrian, Yank, Parker, and Noah kept up an undying poker game.

With surprising speed for such a large man, George

was into the neighboring tent. Tommy and Zeb sprinted after him. In seconds, George had his long arms wrapped tightly around Jeff's chest, holding him away from Adrian. Tommy saw Adrian's eyes narrow to menacing slits. "You'd better get him out of here fast. I don't take kindly to words like that, even from a liquored-up coward."

"*Coward!*" Jeff stopped struggling for a moment, his eyes going wide with shock. His short laugh was an ugly sound. "Very clever! Call a man a name and take his mind off the real issue. Well, it won't work! No man can be as lucky as you've been without cheating."

"If anyone's a cheat, it's you," Adrian taunted. "You claimed to know all there is to know about wingwalking, but you sure haven't been anxious to show us your act. And I notice it's George and not you who's been practicing with Tommy."

Jeff's face had gone very pale. Before he could answer, Zeb stepped between them. "That's just about enough. You men are mighty lucky Miz Kelly flew out to check on our next town. If she'd heard this ruckus, you'd both be fired. And prob'ly the rest of you, too." His sharp eyes studied the money piled in the table's center. "Looks like these stakes have gone a bit higher than penny ante."

Zeb bent to pick up an empty liquor bottle. "And the refreshments are a mite stronger than Miz Kelly allows, too." Zeb's gaze traveled around the table. "Well, what about it? Was it an honest game?"

Noah broke the long silence with a nervous chuckle. "Well, it sure did seem almost magical the way Adrian was pulling the right cards. Yank and me was near picked clean. I was just fixin' to quit when Jeff broke loose."

Parker's smooth voice intruded. "Gentlemen, I lost as much, if not more, than any of you tonight, but I'm sure cheating had nothing to do with it. When a man's lucky star gets to shining like that, we should know enough to quit early." With a rueful shrug he fingered the few bills left on the table in front of him, then scooped them into his hat. "Let's call it a night and have no more name-calling."

Shamefaced, the other players picked up their few remaining dollars and left. George stuffed Jeff's money into his pocket and pulled him from the tent. Only Adrian was unhurried as he spread his jacket on a chair, then swept the enormous pile of winnings into it, and gathered it up by the edges. He sneered at Zeb, "I reckon when Ted and Cynthia get back, you'll have to tattle-tale, won't you?"

Zeb shrugged. "I won't have to tell her nothin'. She can smell trouble. She'll have the whole story out of the first fella she sees."

They all turned in for the night, but it took Tommy a long time to get to sleep. He kept thinking how different an air show was from the way he'd imagined it. Just as he dozed off, Tommy thought of Zeb's words on the night he had run away from home: *Don't come crying to me when you find out the world out there ain't perfect neither.*

It seemed Tommy had been asleep only a few minutes when he was wakened by a sharp "Crack!" just outside his tent. It was followed by a harsh whisper, "Jeez, you got a full moon. Can't you watch where you step?" Tommy recognized Adrian's voice.

Parker's voice answered. "If I wasn't lugging so much of your gear, I could see better!"

Quickly Tommy tiptoed over to peer through the crack in the tent entrance. Yank's snore continued uninterrupted. Outside, the silhouette of the Canuck was outlined in the moonlight, and after a moment, Tommy realized that Parker and Adrian were loading it with supplies.

"We'll never get all this in there with us," Adrian hissed.

"So leave it," Parker whispered back. "With what we skinned from those suckers, we can buy anything we need."

Adrian chuckled. "The dopes were watching me so close, you could have dealt yourself a whole extra hand."

Parker gave his little yip laugh. "Let's get this thing moved to the end of the runway." Stealthily the two began to push the airplane toward its takeoff point.

Tommy's hands were clenched. "I've got to stop them!" he thought. "But I'll need help." Yank was no use; he took forever to wake up. And Zeb was too old. Then Tommy remembered George's grip on Jeff. And Jeff was no weakling either. If he could just get to their tent . . . He would have to run across behind the Canuck, but Adrian and Parker were facing the other way.

Barefoot, Tommy sped across the damp grass. His progress was silent—until he reached the point where Adrian and Parker had loaded the plane. Suddenly his feet tangled in something. Trying to muffle his cry, he fell heavily to the ground.

Parker whirled. "It's that stupid kid! Shut him up fast

before he wakes everyone up!"

Tommy was almost back on his feet. He saw the punch that Adrian was aiming at his chin and groggily decided to duck away from it. But even as he made the decision, the blow connected. Tommy felt his head snap back, there was intense pain, and then he was sinking, sprawling down on top of the pile of castoff possessions that Adrian and Parker had left behind.

Chapter
14

SOMEONE—HE THOUGHT IT WAS ZEB—WAS HOLDING COLD compresses to Tommy's bruised chin. He came to reluctantly, his mind aware not just of pain but of a strong sense of defeat. Lying on his own cot, he stared up at the anxious faces above him and imagined he heard a faint echo of the Canuck's engine fading in the distance.

"They got away!" He found he was speaking through cut and swelling lips.

Noah patted his shoulder. "And good riddance to them. As long as you're all right kid, there couldn't be a better thing happen to this show than to see the last of those rascals."

"But they cheated you—they took all your money!"

Noah grinned down at him. "Oh, I never really put *all* my money into a game, Tom. That's *one* thing Yank and I learned in the Army."

"Well, they got every cent of mine, the dirty so-and-sos," Jeff raged.

George put an arm across Jeff's shoulders. "I'll tell you what, partner—I'll give you half of my bankroll. It's worth it not to be spending the next couple of weeks keeping you and that cardsharp separated."

Jeff punched a fist into the palm of his other hand. "I could have done a nice rearranging job on that pretty face, if you'd kept your hands off me."

"Ah, but remember, Jefferson, in the meantime *he* might have landed a lucky punch or two. And then where'd we be—with only *our* ugly mugs to attract the ladies?"

Zeb's drawl broke into the laughter. "Reckon we might as well crawl back into bed for a few hours 'til it gets light. Then, while we wait for Miz Kelly, we can clean up this mess and work on our rehearsin'."

"How we going to rehearse with no announcer?" Yank muttered.

Tommy raised his head, wincing with pain at the sudden movement. "Jeff! Jeff can do the announcing. He had a great spiel when I heard him last summer."

Jeff struggled to conceal his relief. "Well, I'd certainly be glad to try it—that is, if George doesn't mind taking on the . . . performing."

George shrugged and winked at Tommy. "I got such a good teacher, I'm bound to become a star."

"And wait'll you guys see the new routine Yank and I been thinking up!" Noah bragged. "Why, the show's going to be better than ever!"

Tommy was the first to spot them when Mrs. Kelly and Teddy flew back into camp late the next morning.

He called to the others, and everyone hurried over to watch the Standard land and taxi to its parking place. It seemed to Tommy that the propeller had barely stopped revolving before all the men began to talk at once.

Cynthia Kelly threw up her hands. "Heavens! Zeb, *you* tell me what happened. The rest of you, please *be quiet!*"

Zeb's story was brief, but complete. Mrs. Kelly—her lips pressed tight, her eyes angry—insisted on examining Tommy's bruises and cuts. "Thank goodness you weren't badly hurt! I *knew* I should have fired them before. They've meant trouble ever since they got together. Adrian alone could cause mischief, but he wasn't smart enough to start cheating at cards. *I* had to hire Parker to help him!"

"We all agreed to Parker, Miz Kelly," Teddy reminded her. "You can't blame yourself."

Yank was optimistic. "I think getting rid of those two was a lucky break. Why, the show we've whipped up is a lot better!"

Tommy saw a quick glance pass from Teddy to Mrs. Kelly that she answered with an almost imperceptible shake of her head. She looked around at the troupe, a half smile replacing her frown. "So you think we won't have to cancel?"

"Don't forget you have us," Jeff thumped his chest and pointed to George. "Your replacements were here before you even needed them!"

George added, "We may not know all the routines perfectly yet, but if you'll cut the fanciest bits, I think we can fill in."

Mrs. Kelly hesitated, and she had to clear her throat

before she spoke. "This means a lot to me, boys, more than you can imagine. We have just one more show scheduled for this town. It would have gone against my grain not to be able to meet the contract."

She straightened, taking command. "All right, let's get going! We have just enough time to dress and run through one quick rehearsal before the crowd arrives." She glanced again at Teddy. "We'll make this a last performance that people will never forget!"

The members of the troupe turned away, but Mrs. Kelly called Tommy back. "Are you sure you feel up to this today, Tom?"

"Oh sure, ma'am. George is going to go up with me, the way we've been doing when we practice. He'll do some of the stunts. The only thing in the act I won't be able to handle is that big smile." Tommy pointed to his swollen lips and attempted a tiny, cautious grin.

A few hours later he watched as the stands filled with spectators. On the platform Jeff was keeping a close eye on the sky to the east where four planes circled. Exactly at the scheduled time, he stepped forward and signaled for attention.

Jeff's honeyed tones were different from the harsher salesmanship Parker had used. "Welcome, welcome, everyone! What a lovely town this is. I tell you, all of us are sad today, knowing that this will be our last show here. Never have we played to such knowledgable people. Obviously you are aware that we have entered into a new Air Age. And, by attending this performance, you have shown that you appreciate the skilled pilots who are leading us into our future. A future where airplanes will be as common a way to travel as the automobiles in which you have arrived!"

An indignant snort arose from an elderly farmer seated near Tommy. "*I* didn't come in no trashy automobile," he objected. "My buggy will still be around when fads like these here horseless carriages and flying machines have been outlawed. Easy ways to kill yerself—that's all they are!" His embarrassed daughter shushed him in time for those around to hear the last words of Jeff's introduction.

". . . Without further ado, the *world renowned Kelly Flying Circus!*" On these last words, Jeff raised his hand. At once a green flare fired from behind the platform and blazed a high arc into the sky. The four planes quickly arranged themselves into formation and flew toward the platform. Tommy was happy to see that the red and silver Jenny, flown by George, made an eye-catching lead ship, and the airplanes were maintaining a tight formation as they swooped low in front of the grandstand.

Noah and Yank seemed to be having no trouble keeping up with George, as they had had with Adrian. And when these three began their time-consuming climb for altitude, Teddy's sneak maneuver around behind the crowd and sudden buzz job still proved an excellent distraction. Tommy chuckled as even those he knew had seen the show before couldn't stop themselves from ducking.

The performers were maintaining a good pace. While Teddy was doubling back to begin the demonstration of controlled flying, Jeff displayed the bright handkerchief, then helped Mrs. Kelly place it on the end of the pole. In his first pass Teddy missed the crimson bandana, but he circled back at once for another try. On the second approach, he caught it neatly on his left wing tip. With a triumphant roar the Standard swept away into a quick, banking turn.

The eyes of the other watchers were following the airplane, but Tommy's gaze was on Mrs. Kelly as she made ready for the new stunt that she and Teddy had worked out. She was balancing a light, woven straw basket on the end of the bamboo rod. Teddy returned, thundering nearer and nearer to Mrs. Kelly while Jeff kept up an excited commentary. This time Teddy was successful on the first try. The audience broke into cheers when the huge plane lowered its right wing and a hook attached there plucked the basket from the pole so daintily that the rod barely swayed.

As the applause died, Tommy could hear Jeff saying, "Now our Master of Precision would like to present a gift to all of the lovely ladies in our audience." Teddy's turnaround this time was quite different from his others. He flew in a wide circle, staying almost level. He was higher, and cautious about keeping the right wing from dipping—until the moment he started back over the crowd. Then he tipped the wing steeply, the basket flew, and a shower of fresh flowers sprinkled down upon the delighted spectators.

Jeff had a natural flair for timing, Tommy noticed. He allowed the recipients plenty of time to admire the flowers they had caught. But the moment their chatter began to die, he directed their attention upward.

High above, the mock dogfight had begun. Yank and

Noah were flying with incomparable skill. Tommy caught his breath when they seemed to pass just inches apart in their daring maneuvers. Never had they left themselves so little margin for error! The spectators sensed this and cheered the pilots on. After Yank's final victory, the applause was loud and enthusiastic.

George, following at once with the sequence of loops, did not fare as well. The response from those watching became more and more disinterested. "I was glad to see that Kraut get shot down," Tommy heard a young man in the stands mutter, "but who cares how many times an airplane can loop? I just get bored counting."

When George leveled off, there was only light clapping. Yank, who had come to stand beside Tommy after he landed, said, "See? I told you we needed something really new. Wait until they see this!" He hurried over to the platform and made a great ceremony of handing a piece of paper up to Mrs. Kelly. She read it and whirled to tap Jeff on the shoulder. He interrupted his speech, scanned through the paper, and then waved it over his head.

"Ladies and gentlemen," Jeff announced, "we have just received wonderful news! Miss Carol LeFarr, the lovely Hollywood actress, has been visiting here in the East and is actually at the fair right now. Our own Lieutenant Minelli, whom you just saw outfly and overwhelm his German adversary, has begged for the honor of taking Miss LeFarr for a ride. And she has agreed!"

Jeff and Mrs. Kelly started the applause, and the watchers joined in as each of them twisted his head this way and that, looking for the celebrity. Few would have admitted, Tommy suspected, that they had never before heard the actress's name.

The audience was not left in doubt long about where the motion picture queen was. Yank, his uniform sparkling with meaningless medals and ribbons, marched proudly back to the dressing tent, bowed, and held out his hand to draw forth—Noah!

Even though Tommy knew it was Noah in the outlandish costume, he felt a twinge of disbelief. Why would he volunteer to wear that make-up and slinky red gown with its well-placed padding? Where had he found the unnaturally yellow curls that danced below the edges of his regular flying helmet?

Noah's inexperience with high-heeled, silver strap shoes caused the "beauty" to mince with charming delicacy toward the waiting airplane. Once there, Miss Le-Farr bowed and waved with great enthusiasm to those who applauded.

The Lieutenant was careful to stand so that the lady's rather unshapely legs were concealed as she climbed into the forward cockpit. As soon as she was settled and absorbed in throwing kisses to her public, Yank climbed into the rear seat. He signaled to Zeb, who started the pull-through on the prop.

After giving a few false coughs, the engine roared to life. Lieutenant Yank reduced the speed of the motor to idle. Then, unexpectedly, he seemed to remember something. He leaped back out of his cockpit and ran toward the tent.

"Just a minute, folks, just a minute," Jeff was announcing in a soothing voice. "I believe the Lieutenant has forgotten his lucky rabbit's foot, which he has carried on every flight throughout the war and since. Please be patient—he'll be back with us in a moment. Oh! ... Oh, wait a minute! Miss LeFarr, Miss LeFarr, no! Don't touch that throttle. That makes the motor go faster. The plane will start to move!"

Chapter

15

THE PLANE DID BEGIN TO MOVE, WHILE SEVERAL WOMEN in the stands screamed in fright. Zeb acted out attempts to stop it by making awkward, blundering reaches for the wings and then the tail. Yank came running out portraying desperation and fear as he chased the careening Jenny around the field.

Twice the runaway machine swerved in, seeming certain to plow into the front rows of spectators' seats. Tommy was amazed at the agility of the people seated there. Young or old, they leaped away toward the upper tiers. Each time, by what seemed incredible luck, the plane veered in another direction at the last possible moment.

Finally still weaving from side to side, the aircraft turned toward the runway, while the actress waved helpless hands and implored someone to save her. The ship began to gather more and more speed—so much that it was obvious it would soon leave the ground. On the take-off the Jenny teetered as if a drunken person were flying it. It narrowly avoided ground looping, one wing dragging dangerously close to the earth.

By this time several spectators seemed close to fainting, and the whole audience was spellbound with horror as they watched the ship wobble higher and higher. Then— in an instant—the weaving aircraft recovered from its awkward bumbling and began to fly beautifully. Tommy expelled the breath he had been holding since that near-disastrous takeoff. Thank Heavens! Noah had stopped maneuvering the ship with his knees and had brought his hands to rest on the set of controls in the front seat.

Tommy could feel the conflicting emotions in the people around him as they watched Noah go on to perform a series of low level aerobatics. Some were still shaken, some were looking sheepish, and a few seemed angry at the way they had been tricked. He too was having a hard time deciding how he felt about this act. He admired—and envied—the expert way Noah was coaxing amazing feats from the temperamental Jenny. But the way he'd introduced these aerobatics was something else again.

When the "actress" landed, she flounced away from the airplane to step onto the platform. Helping herself to Jeff's megaphone, she cooed in falsetto, "Pooh, what's so hard about flying!" Apparently deciding to take off her helmet and wave it at the watchers, she pretended to be unaware when the golden wig came off also. That broke the ice with the audience. They laughed and applauded while Noah took bow after bow and then made a triumphant exit.

Tommy, waiting to start the finale, avoided Noah's eyes when he wobbled past. "He told me once he'd be the clown of this circus," Tommy reminded himself. "And he *was* funny." But there was something wrong. Fragments of comments made during the performance returned to Tommy's ears.

". . . Sit down, *please*, Pa! Doc would have a fit if he knew you'd been jumping around like that with your bad heart!"

". . . I *knew* it—anyone that takes a ride in one of them things is asking for trouble!"

". . . Any durn fool who gets himself up like a woman ain't gonna lead *me* into the future—or anywhere else!"

This last had won loud guffaws from the speaker's cronies. But Tommy had clenched his fists in anger. Why couldn't the man see what was important—Noah's bravery and skill?

"That's it!" The realization came to Tommy as he stared after Noah. "If we take chances like that, if we act so crazy, how can we expect people to trust us—or our airplanes!"

There was no time to pursue the thought. Jeff was beginning another introduction. ". . . a battle to determine —once and for all—the world's greatest aerial stunt man." Tommy winced. It was his turn now to play the fool. His steps dragged toward the Standard.

Reaching down from the rear cockpit, Mrs. Kelly offered him a hand up. As he squeezed with George into the front seat, Tommy remembered the doubts she had once expressed. But Captain Kelly's idea of air exhibitions *had* been a good one! When had it gone wrong? Tommy brushed a hand across his forehead, as if to sweep away his thoughts. He must concentrate on the performance.

They were off and climbing, Mrs. Kelly soon banking into a circle that would bring them back in front of the grandstand. Moving swiftly, but with caution, the two stunt men climbed out to stand on either side of the fuselage. Below, Tommy knew that Jeff would be playing up their competition as they began what looked like an airborne game of Follow the Leader.

First, Tommy worked his way to the top of the upper wing and took his usual stance with legs spread wide, hands on hips, and head high. After several minutes he struggled back to the front cockpit and George edged his way forward to imitate the stunt. When George went further and performed the headstand, he made the extra move seem a challenge.

Accepting the dare, Tommy moved out to hang by both hands from the left wing skid. While he still dangled there, George inched out onto the right wing and swung down to hang by his hands from that skid. There the two of them clung, as Mrs. Kelly flew them around in front of the onlookers.

It was incredible, thought Tommy that she maintained a flight so stable in spite of the way they had moved around. What a marvelous pilot she was! He threw a wry grin at his fellow stunt man. With Mrs. Kelly's skill—and Zeb's harnesses—to protect them, the two might live to tell their grandchildren about all this foolishness.

Tommy was careful to avoid catching his arms in the safety wires when he swung down into a knee hang. Through his whipping scarf he caught glimpses of George, who was again following his lead. They had planned to point up their rivalry by throwing defiant waves at each other while they hung upside down. Tommy, looking at the upturned melon faces below, shook his fist. But the gesture was not aimed at George. It was for anyone down there who was hoping they would get careless.

Back up on the wings, they moved toward the fuselage, and the last, most dangerous part of their act. George had not yet practiced the hay drop, but he watched as Tommy went through careful preparation—crawling down onto the spreader bar, hanging by his knees as he judged the approaching target, and falling at last into the center of the waiting hay mound.

Mrs. Kelly flew around again while George crawled down between the wheels, positioned his knees over the axle, and looked as if he too were preparing to drop. But, at the last moment he righted himself, climbed back up to the front cockpit, and plumped into the seat. With greatly exaggerated motions, he folded his arms and firmly shook his head. When Mrs. Kelly flew past the audience once more, he held up a large sign. Giant letters, drawn hastily that morning, read "I QUIT!" And on the ground Tommy ran out to take one more bow as Jeff pronounced him "the winner and still champion among stunt men!"

The crowd seemed fairly happy with the improvised performance, and many were lining up to purchase tickets. But Jeff's voice grew hoarse as he tried to persuade more spectators to buy.

"Come on, ladies and gentlemen. This is your last chance before we must go on to our next location. Come and ride with Captain Winslow. Or—I, myself, Jeff Johnson, will take you in my specially built stunt aircraft."

Listening from the dressing tent, George shook his head and glanced at Tommy. "The only thing special about that Jenny of ours is the paint job. I think it's what holds the crate together. Jeff never wants to spend a cent on maintenance. I can tell you now—I wasn't sure it would make it through that consecutive loops stunt."

Tommy shot him a startled look. "Why did you risk it?"

George shrugged. "How could I refuse and lose out on the first decent food we've had in months? Haven't you heard that joke that's going around? 'What's the most dangerous part of barnstorming for a living?' "

Tommy shook his head. "What's the answer?"

George grinned. "Starving to death!" His face sobered as he listened to Jeff almost begging the customers to try a ride with him. "Jeff hasn't really enjoyed introducing the stars instead of being one," he said grimly. A moment later, his head jerked up. "What's that? What's he saying?"

Tommy too, had been alerted by a strange new tone in Jeff's voice. The announcer was saying, "Can I take you up and do a loop? Why, son, I can do everything but turn that plane inside out. It'll cost you two tickets, though."

George and Tommy jumped to their feet. Mrs. Kelly

had a strict rule—no aerobatics with passengers. They ran outside. Jeff and a lanky young farmhand were already climbing into the striped Jenny, at the far end of the line of ships.

"Buckle up tight, friend," Jeff called out. "We'll go up there and give people a real show—let 'em have a chance to read my name! Come on, Yank, give us a pull-through."

They couldn't hear Yank's answer, but Jeff's high, excited tones came clearly. "Too late to tell me now. A promise is a promise. And I already collected!"

George began to run toward the plane, but he was too late. Yank, shrugging, had given the prop one pull-through, and the motor started up at once. In minutes, the sparkling stripes were flashing in the late afternoon sun as the Jenny taxied across the field, swung into position, and took off.

Tommy saw Mrs. Kelly emerge from the office tent. Her face was grim as she watched Jeff coaxing the Jenny to climb at its best speed. The ship seemed to sense his impatience, and like most of her kind, responded with exasperating, "I-will-not-be-rushed" deliberation.

Finally, Jeff leveled off. Teddy turned to reassure Mrs. Kelly. "He's not really going to do it. See? He's too low to try a loop. He's just going to give the fella a regular ride."

The others in the troupe looked relieved, but Tommy's eyes were drawn to George. "Oh no," George croaked as he clenched and unclenched his fists. "I told him not to trust that altimeter. The darn fool, can't he see he's not high enough?"

A sudden tense silence was shared by performers and

watching townspeople. The red and silver aircraft seemed to hesitate for a moment. Then Jeff pointed its nose toward the ground in the steep dive needed to build up enough air speed to bring the plane up, over onto its back, and on around in a complete circle.

The watchers could hear the wind singing through the wing wires as the ship dropped faster and faster. Yank murmured in awe, "You know, I think he can make it. He just might make it if he pulls out now."

As if Jeff had heard him, the controlling surfaces on the craft moved to bring the ship out of the dive. Slowly, very slowly, she responded as the earth rose to meet her with terrifying speed.

Tommy actually heard the soft swish as the Jenny at last pulled up, her wheels parting tall grass stems in the pasture next to the fairground. Then she was climbing, climbing, continuing the circle until both her occupants hung upside down from their seat belts at the top of the loop. The control surfaces moved again and the Jenny went into a half-roll, bringing her passengers right side up.

"Look at that! An Immelman!" Yank sounded almost reverent. "He's either insane or—brilliant!"

Noah's answer was terse. "That's one way to make it look planned."

Jeff was flying cautiously now. His slow turns and let-down were models of propriety, and his landing was flawless. When he taxied in to park, the townspeople clapped and cheered wildly, and he eagerly accepted their praise. But Tommy was certain that none of the performers envied him—they knew what Mrs. Kelly would have to say.

Tommy dropped onto a nearby bleacher. The churning emotions of the past hour had left him feeling weak and drained. He didn't see the man on the bicycle until he heard someone say, "Tommy Davison?" and looked up at a chubby man in a Western Union hat, holding an envelope toward him.

Still numb, Tommy opened the envelope and gazed at the brief words. *Tommy. Pap fell and hurt bad. We need you. Mark.*

Chapter

16

THE TELEGRAM CRACKLED IN HIS POCKET WHEN TOMMY, leaving the Ohio to follow the Allegheny River north, turned Mrs. Kelly's Jenny into a slight left bank. Questions the wire had raised dinned over and over in Tommy's mind. "How badly hurt is Pap? Not . . . not *dying? No*, Pap's a strong man—he'll pull out of whatever it is. . . . How long will they need me? If Pap's crippled, there's no way Mark can run the farm alone Am I going to end up a farmer after all?"

Grateful to Teddy, who had let him handle the controls since takeoff, Tommy tried to concentrate on making each move precise and perfect. He did not want to hear the other question at the back of his mind, "Will this be the last time I ever fly an airplane?"

He glanced around, willing himself to fix the cockpit in his memory so that he would never forget it. He listened to the song the winds played on the reinforcing wires, and even held up his face to smell and memorize the odors of gasoline and oil.

"*Already?*" The word stabbed unbidden through his mind when Anna's Corner appeared on the horizon. Immediately he was ashamed. In another few minutes they were over the WILLIS LIVERY STABLE & *Garage*. There was Mr. Burvin's barbershop—and Doc's house—and the school.

A strange sensation filled Tommy. As he saw each familiar building, he had the feeling he was shrinking, that he was turning back into the boy the people below remembered. Even now it was hard to believe that he had walked the wings of this airplane, had repaired its engine and all the others in the Kelly fleet, had tackled many strange and difficult jobs in an adult world—and proved himself capable.

Tommy thought how different this homecoming was from the one he had dreamed of. How happy he would be if it were as he had planned—he in his own airplane, independent and successful, ready to prove to his father that a man could make an honest living from flying! Leaning over the side to study the upcoming fields of his father's farm, he lifted his goggles and let the wind blow tears into his eyes.

"The north pasture looks pretty good," he shouted back to Teddy. "And it's the most level. Want to set her down there?"

Teddy shrugged and answered, "You're drivin', kid. Whatever pleases you just tickles me plumb to death."

Tommy squared his shoulders. The feeling of shrinking was gone. Teddy had given him back at least a part of his dream. No one could turn the man he had become back into a child. People would realize that when they saw that he was now a trusted pilot.

He circled low over the field, studying it for hidden rocks or gullies. As they came on around over the house, Mark burst from the barn, his upturned face lit by a beaming smile. A moment later Ma bustled out the kitchen door, whipping off her flowered apron to wave it joyfully over her head.

Tommy noticed Ma's wash pinned out on the back line. It hung limp. Good, there was no wind to worry about. He circled, slowing down, following each step just as Mrs. Kelly had taught him. Steady, steady now, and they were down in a perfect landing. When they rolled to a stop, Teddy called out, "Can't be done any better than that!" As if he'd been reading Tommy's mind, he said, "You're a born flier, Tom. Don't worry, you'll get back to airplanes one day—I haven't a doubt of it!"

Tommy unbuckled his seat belt and climbed onto the wing, then jumped to the ground. Mark had stopped a few feet short of the airplane, and Tommy looked across—no, now he had to look *up*—into his brother's face. "How's Pap?" he asked.

Mark's nod was reassuring as he closed the distance between them. "Pap'll be better in no time now—he's fretted so about whether you were all right." He took Tommy's hand in a crunching grasp. "Golly, it's good to have you home again!"

Ma stumbled up to the Jenny, her face red from the exertion of running across the field. "Oh . . . oh, Tommy!" was all she could manage to say, but her eyes shone. She threw her arms around him.

It took Mark's curious stare to remind Tommy of Teddy, still seated in the Jenny. With one arm around his mother, he turned quickly and said, "Ma, Mark—this is Teddy. Step down, Ted, and shake hands with my *baby* brother." He laughed, reaching up to pat Mark's red curls. "And Ma here is the best cook in the county. Won the prizes to prove it. Come on in and eat supper with us."

Teddy reached down to shake Mark's hand and sent an apologetic glance toward Ma. "This fellow sure makes it hard for me to do my duty, ma'am, but Miz Kelly needs me back as fast as I can make it. There's an awful lot to be done when you're breaking up ... uh ... moving an air show." He glanced at the sun. "I figure if I leave right now, I'll be back to camp a little before sundown. Sure glad I had a chance to meet you folks. I'll take you up on that supper another time."

Regretfully, Tommy nodded. "Okay, Ted, we'll hold you to that." He knew Teddy was needed. It had been a great kindness for Mrs. Kelly to spare him so that Tommy could get home as fast as possible. Leading Ma and Mark back to a safe distance, Tommy returned to prop the Jenny. Before he moved to the front of the airplane, he reached up to shake Teddy's hand.

"We'll miss you, Tom," Teddy said gruffly. "You carried your own weight—and then some." He cleared his throat. "I sure hope your pa gets better fast."

Tommy wished he were better at pretty speeches. There was so much he'd like to say. But all that came out was, "Thanks, Ted ... for everything." He whirled and went to the propeller. When he started to call, "Switch off?" he found he had to swallow several times before he could make the words come out.

As soon as the Jenny was off the ground and headed away, the three Davisons began to walk toward the farmhouse. Tommy looked at Ma and spoke the words he had dreaded, "How bad is Pap?"

Her smile faded, and he saw the many new worry lines that creased her forehead. "He's better, Tommy. He's going to be all right. It's just that it will take a long time, and you know your pa's not a patient man."

Tommy was struggling with impatience himself. "Well, what *happened?*" he demanded. "Mark's telegram didn't explain a thing."

"Your pa was determined to paint the house—all by himself. Mark said he'd help, soon as he could, but Bert is so stubborn. He won't admit he's not as steady on a ladder as he once was. And—I think once he gave in and hired Smiley with the money you left, he was determined to do somethin' extra around here.

"Anyway," Ma continued with a sigh, "he was about halfway through—as you can see—and was near to the top rung when the ladder started sliding off where he had it resting against the roof. I seen him start to go and tried to run, but I was too late. He rode that ladder clear to the ground—couldn't seem to think to jump clear." Ma's eyes filled with tears. "When I got to him, he was moaning awful, in terrible pain. I knew for sure he'd broke something."

"I got Doc here as fast as I could," Mark went on. "He found one arm broke—a clean break and easy to set." Tommy looked puzzled and opened his mouth, but Mark was already answering his unspoken question. "The bad news was the other arm, the left one. It was shattered at the elbow. Poor Pap finally fainted before Doc got it set, and we're praying all the pieces went where they're supposed to be. But it's going to be a long time before Pap can use it, even so."

"Both arms in casts!"

Mark nodded. "It's been powerful hard on him and on Ma, too. She's worn herself out feeding him, washing him, and all. I've tried to help, but I couldn't just let the crops go, and of course, Smiley isn't much at going ahead on his own."

Ma spoke softly as they neared the house. "We didn't send for you just because we need your help, Tommy, though that's certainly God's truth. But when your pa was worst sick, the first days, he kept muttering about you being in danger. He was out of his head some—and he'd talk and talk about how sorry he was he'd not let you do what you wanted to."

Tommy could not help the look of amazement that crossed his face, and Ma saw it. She stopped and faced her two sons, a sudden determination on her face. "There's something I never told you boys. Never meant to tell you. . . . But maybe it will make it easier for you to put up with the way Pap gets. Maybe you'll see why he sometimes just has to . . . get away from here for a while."

Hesitating, she stared down at her hands, one clenched tightly around the other. "You see, Pap never wanted to be a farmer." Mark's eyes widened with surprise, but Tommy felt a new understanding for his father.

"You ever noticed," Ma went on in a tired voice, "how your pa's face will look when we hear a train whistle?" Both boys shook their heads. "Well, *I* see it, and it near breaks my heart. Bert had big dreams once, too. He was as crazy about trains as you are about airplanes, Tommy. But *his* pa said he had no right leavin' a farm that would be his someday. And your father had to stay. Your grandpa did need him—he didn't have any other sons." Tommy flushed, but Ma didn't seem to notice.

"Bert hasn't done bad with the farm, but his heart ain't in it. And sometimes he gets mad at the whole world because he's stuck here. Then, when he was so sick, he kept saying, 'I done my own boy just like my pa done me! I wanted to stick him with farmin' just cause I'd had to do it. I should've understood. I should've helped him. And now he's in danger! I feel it. I feel it!' "

Mark said, "It made the hair on the back of my neck stand up the way he'd say that about you. Finally I just got me into Middleton and sent that wire." Mark searched Tommy's face. "Was there any truth to it, Tom? Were you doing something dangerous?"

"*Emma! Mark!*" Pap's roar from above saved Tommy from answering. "Where in the devil is everybody? By Jehosophat, if I could just get up by myself, I'd find out what's going on around here. I got a good notion to try rolling out. I'll find out what the blazes all that noise is in the pasture . . ."

Tommy hurried into the bedroom just as Pap made a determined lunge, trying to roll onto his right side. His face went white with pain, and he flopped back. Then he saw Tommy standing in the doorway. His frustrated cursing stopped. "Tommy!" he choked. "Oh, Tommy!"

Not conscious of having moved, Tommy found himself kneeling by the bedside, his head on his father's chest, while Pap tried to hug him in spite of the two casts. It was a long time before Pap cleared his throat and got back to his normal tones. " 'Bout time you had sense enough to come home where you belong!" he muttered.

Chapter

17

"CONSARN IT! TOM! MARK! ROLL OUTA THOSE BEDS AND
get movin'. I gotta show you the row of peas you
missed yesterday. You musta been pickin' with your
eyes closed. If 'twasn't for me checkin', there'd be as
much wasted as gathered around here."

At Pap's first shout from downstairs, Tommy and
Mark were up and reaching for the overalls that hung
on their bedposts. Tommy grinned over at Mark. It felt
good, he thought, to be old enough to realize that Pap's
grumbling was just his way. His fierceness meant no
more than the wild barking the Miller's dog set up when
anyone came near.

Throughout each of the long July days they had
worked steadily, but never hard and fast enough for
their father. Pap's brusque orders sometimes irritated
Tommy. But when he studied Pap's face above the two

dirty gray casts, he knew what Mark said was true, "He's hollerin' more to shout down the pain than to whip us up."

Tommy had been home for nearly a month. The day after he returned, Mark had been dejected as he showed his brother several fields. "Put in more hay than real cash crops. Pap wasn't sure enough of Smiley. Thought we wouldn't have enough help to keep anything else hoed. And I never got the north field planted at all. Too big."

"Never mind, Mark," Tommy had reassured him. "We'll just take extra good care of the cash crops you did plant."

Tommy also volunteered to complete painting the house. He told his family that it was a real holiday for him to climb around on something that held still. Joking like this about life with the air circus, he found himself implying that the stunts he had done were simple ones. In a similar style, he glossed over the treachery of Adrian and Parker and the way Jeff had cheated the undertaker by the length of a blade of grass.

What Tommy spoke of most was the pure joy of flying. So enthusiastic was he that even Ma began to plan for the day when Tommy would have his very own airplane. Only Pap ridiculed the "foolishness of such dreaming." Tommy maintained a smiling composure. "Wait and see, Pap. The day will come when I bring an airplane home. And when I say, 'Who's first?' you'll be at the head of the line."

But when he lay awake at night, Tommy forced himself to face reality. With the limited planting, money would be tight for his folks this year. If any farming plagues hit—drought, cows going dry, or fierce storms just when the crops needed sun—well, his parents would need help.

One night shortly after he'd come home, Tommy had offered Pap the savings he'd built up. "Lord Almighty, no, boy!" Pap had exploded. "I may have two broken arms, but I'm still able to provide for my own. We've been through lean times before. If you'll just put your back into these everlasting chores, we'll not need to take your money too."

Pap continued to glare, but softened his voice and, for just a moment, allowed the unbandaged tips of his fingers to rest on Tommy's arm. "I'm already beholden for what you give us in the past. There's still a bit of that left to keep Smiley on."

Pap's voice went back to loud. "Well, come on now, let's get us some rest. I swear to Gabriel I can hear them weeds growing in the cornfields. You and Mark will have to get to hoeing out there at first light."

Now Pap was inside eating breakfast while Tommy and Mark were once again working with their hoes. It was good, Tommy thought, to enjoy these first quiet minutes before their father came out and began flinging orders. The boys knew why he always waited to eat until later. Pap could not bear for anyone to see how Ma had to feed him as if he were a tiny child.

Just as he reached the end of a row, Tommy thought he heard something, a noise so familiar that he felt a squeezing sensation in his chest. He willed himself not to look up until he saw Mark stop and raise his head. Then Tommy was sure he was not imagining, and he scanned the sky quickly.

The plane was low as it came over the southern horizon. Tommy identified it—a Standard, and by the sound of it, one with a Hisso engine. Mrs. Kelly's? No, he could see now that the color was wrong, and there was a strange device painted on this ship's side. The insignia looked like a giant tobacco pouch. As the plane circled lower, he read out the huge letters on the pouch's side, "U. S. MAIL."

"Well, I'll be durned," said Mark. "I've heard of them mailplanes in the East, but what's one doing out here?"

"I don't know," Tommy replied, "but if he isn't planning to land in the north field, he sure believes in low sightseeing!"

Just as the plane touched down, Pap came hurrying out the kitchen door. Ma followed him as far as the porch steps. "Bert, you know Doc warned you about falling again!" Her husband ignored her as he hastened out to confront the intruders. Tommy and Mark edged closer, their hoeing mere motions as they watched and listened with interest.

The plane taxied to a stop near their father and two men climbed out. The first was dressed in usual pilot's garb—warm jacket, jodhpurs, boots, and helmet with goggles. This man turned to help the other one step to the ground.

It was evident that the second gentleman was not at home in the skies. He wore a business suit, complete with vest and tie, and was hurriedly replacing his helmet with a straw hat. The brim of the straw looked as if it had been clutched a bit too tightly on the journey.

Carrying a shiny black briefcase, the second man walked stiffly toward Pap. "You are Mr. Davison, correct?" Tommy heard him ask. Pap nodded. In a brisk voice the visitor announced, "I am C. G. Smith, head of the western division of the U. S. Air Mail Service." He started to reach out a hand, hesitated when he saw the two casts, and finally settled for touching the tips of Pap's right hand fingers. Mr. Smith gestured vaguely over his shoulders. "This is Max Wheeler."

The pilot grinned at Pap. "What does the other guy look like?" he asked.

Mr. Smith shot him a disapproving glare, but Pap responded amiably. "Well, let's just say he got a thorough going-over."

Mr. Smith cleared his throat noisily. "Mr. Davison, I've come on a matter of important Air Mail Service business. Is there somewhere we might talk?"

Pap took his time answering. After silent consideration he said, "I reckon I can spare a few minutes. Suppose we all go down and take the breeze on the front porch. My Emma'll fetch you some lemonade." He turned to beckon toward the cornfield. "If it's flying we're going to be talking, I s'pose you want to see my son."

Mr. Smith's eyebrows rose. "Your son! Then you are not the Davison who worked with the Kelly show?"

Pap looked indignant. "I got a farm to run! You must have been hearing about my Tom. He's a fine airplane mechanic and a pilot, too. As well as the best stunt man that Kelly outfit ever had."

Overhearing this as he approached, Tommy laughed to himself and shook his head. "That's my pa!" he thought.

"Never says a good word about me unless he thinks I'm out of earshot."

"Tommy. Mark," Papa called out. "This here's Mr. Smith and that's Mr. Wheeler. They say they want to talk business. Let's all go set ourselves down." He swung around as they walked toward the house. "But I warn you right off, Mr. Smith, Tommy can't take on no flying work now. As you see, I'm laid up pretty bad, and I need both my boys to help out here."

"No, you misunderstand me, sir," Smith corrected. "It's not pilots I'm looking for, but landing fields."

"Landing fields! In this country? What in tarnation for?" Pap spoke in astonishment. "Nearest big city is Pittsburgh, and that's over seventy miles away!"

"I'm well aware of that, Mr. Davison." They were mounting the porch steps, and Mr. Smith opened his briefcase. "May I?" He indicated the picnic table. At Pap's nod, Smith settled himself there and began to pull papers from the case. Within minutes, the old board tabletop was covered with maps.

"I'm sure you've heard of our eastern operation, Mr. Davison," Smith began. "Even before the end of the war—since May 15, 1918, to be precise—we've been flying mail between Washington, D.C., Philadelphia, and New York City."

"Yeah, we heard," Pap drawled, "but the word around here was that the mail on the train beat the air mail oftener than not."

Mr. Smith's face reddened, and he seemed to puff out like an aggravated tom turkey. "Absolute falsehoods, sir! It's true we did have some difficulties in the beginning, but the service is fulfilling every expectation now. With the improved airplanes we have on order, we will soon be able to fly the mail across the entire country!"

Hearing his own raised voice, Mr. Smith took a deep breath and came down to a quieter tone. "Indeed, my very purpose for being here is to begin to fulfill that plan." Smoothing out the maps, which were of various scales, he struggled to arrange the ones labeled Illinois, Indiana, Ohio, Pennsylvania, New Jersey, and New York into a natural sequence. When they were anchored on the table, he began to use his fountain pen as a pointer.

"We have already flown pathfinder flights along this route, and we believe it will soon be feasible to have regular air mail service from New York City . . ." (The pen pointed briefly to it before sweeping to the left.) ". . . to Cleveland . . ." (Another sweep.) ". . . and on to Chicago!" (The pen beat a triumphant tattoo on the large black dot that represented the city.)

"You don't say," Pap murmured. He sat studying the maps for several long minutes. Then he said, "Tommy, take a look at this." Tommy leaned over his father's shoulder. "Now, son," Pap went on, "it's been a long time since I had my jography lessons, but seems to me these maps lack a few things. Oh, they show some county and state lines, and cities, and rivers—why here's one even shows a railroad track—but . . . Mr. Wheeler," Pap looked up at the pilot, "ain't there something called the Allegheny Mountains between New York and Cleveland? Don't you and Tommy think it might help them mail fliers to know just where the valleys are, and how high the peaks?"

Max Wheeler gazed at Pap with new respect. "Amen to that, Mr. Davison. We've lost quite a few good men getting that information the hard way. Especially when we were first ordered to scout this route in midwinter!"

Mr. Smith's voice was like a whiplash. "For every great venture, some sacrifices must be made." He was interrupted by the need to accept a glass of lemonade from Ma. "Thank you." The man made a ceremony of turning his back on Wheeler.

"Let us get on to your part of the picture, Mr. Davison. You see, the airplanes—DeHavilands, Jennies, and Standards—we're using at this point haven't the fuel capacity to go nonstop from New York to Cleveland. We'll need refueling stations along the way. And there may be times when bad weather or a need for repairs would force our ships to land."

Smith sat back and smiled at Tommy's father. "That's where you come in. I have made some inquiries around the Pittsburgh area, and the consensus is that your land would suit our purposes admirably. And I was also led to believe that you know something about aircraft. I've been sent here to tell you that the U. S. Government would like to rent a portion of your land as a refueling stop and emergency landing field."

Tommy looked on in disbelief. Could this really be happening? He thought he'd walked away from airplanes—maybe forever. Instead, they were following him home! But his heart sank. The way Pap felt, Tommy reminded himself, he'd be pretty silly to get any hopes up.

Sure enough, Pap was answering as expected. "Naw, Mr. Smith, I don't believe I care for a setup like that. It's true that the north field's the longest, flattest piece of land hereabouts, probably ideal for what you need, but just where would I raise my hay?"

Mark started to speak, "We still got the—" but Pap silenced him with a glance.

"Anyway," Pap went on. "I can just see what would happen. You'd pay me for the use of the field—some little mite—and, next thing you know, my boy here would be doing your repair jobs for free."

"Well," blustered Smith, "if he's as good as you claim, I'm sure we could arrange to hire him as field supervisor."

"At how much?" Pap asked quickly. Smith quoted a figure. "For *both?*" Pap looked insulted. Nervously, Smith raised the amount considerably higher.

"Well, Mr. Smith, put that in writing, and I believe you got a deal." Pap's face became stern as they awkwardly touched fingers again. "And don't forget the clauses about paying for and repairing any damages to my property." Tommy stared at his father in awe. Slowly Pap raised his eyes—and winked!

Obviously relieved to have the interview over, Mr. Smith began to stuff his precious papers into the briefcase. The group left the porch, Max and Tommy striding on ahead. Max was chuckling when they reached the plane. "Your pa is one sharp bargainer, Tom. Do you really know much about planes, or was he just bluffing?"

Tommy grinned. "I know enough to know you'd better let me fix that radiator before you go anywhere. She's been dripping ever since you landed."

"Don't tell me!" said Max. "That fellow in Pittsburgh swore he had it sealed." He held out his hand to shake Tommy's. "Hallelujah! Maybe for once the mail service has hired a ground man who knows what he's doing!"

Chapter

18

"GROUND MAN." THE PHRASE MAX WHEELER HAD USED weeks before had taken on ironic meaning for Tommy. Watching the deHaviland that he had just gassed and inspected taxi away for takeoff, he realized how he envied that pilot his job. Very early in his new career Tommy had been told that U. S. Air Mail pilots could not allow "civilians" either to fly or to ride in their aircraft. Even when the weather and tailwinds had given a flier extra time to relax awhile before tackling the next leg of his flight, Tommy could only talk flying while the mail ship stood before them, ready and tantalizing.

Tommy glanced across the field at the crowd gathered along the roadside. People drifted in long before the scheduled arrival of every mail plane that came by. And, if a plane was late, they waited for hours, just for the pleasure of watching the landing and takeoff. "There's a funny thing," Tommy said to himself. "All the time I was with the show, I never saw people so crazy about flying as they are around here."

He raised his head, listening. "What's wrong with the deHaviland?" he wondered. The drone of its engine had almost faded into silence, but now it seemed to be getting stronger again. Had the pilot turned back? The weather out that way certainly looked clear enough, and Tommy was sure the plane had been in good condition. Yet there was no doubt about it—the sound was increasing. The plane must be returning.

The people on the roadside heard it too and stopped in the middle of leaving to stare at the far hill. Soon the nose of a plane appeared in almost the same spot at which the tail of the mail plane had vanished.

It took only an instant for Tommy to realize that this was not the familiar government plane with its huge mail pouch insignia. It was a Jenny with bright green markings. Tommy listened, then smiled. The engine sound was as recognizable as the paint job. "Mrs. Kelly's!" he exclaimed.

Impudently waggling its wings for the benefit of the crowd, the plane made a full circle of the field, then descended to settle smoothly onto the landing strip. Tommy hurried forward as the pilot leaped from the wing to the ground. He grinned at Tommy's puzzled expression, then raised his goggles.

"George!" Tommy gasped. "What in the world . . . ? How did you . . . ? Gosh, it's good to see you!"

"You better get some traffic signs around here, boy," George announced. "I just brushed wing tips with one of them fancy air mail specials. He sure wasn't on the lookout for anyone else in his sky. I figured it my plain duty to break him of the daydreamin' habit before it gets him into real trouble."

"But how in the world did you find your way up here? And where's *your* Jenny?"

A look of sorrow flashed across George's face. "Well, that's a long story, Tom. And I sure could use a cold drink before I start to tell it."

By the time George was settled in the kitchen with a glass of lemonade and the chicken sandwich Ma had insisted on making for him, the whole Davison family was gathered around to hear his story. Even Pap, after fierce muttering about chores going undone, could not resist sitting down to hear what had happened since Tommy left the air show.

"Well now, Tom, I don't know quite where to begin. I b'lieve you'd left before Mrs. Kelly announced she was closing the show . . ."

"She closed the show!" Tommy repeated in dismay.

"Yup." George nodded. "Had to. These fairground people started a new gimmick. That day she and Teddy come back, they was bringing bad news. Our next town had backed out of their contract. Less, of course, we was willing to *pay* for the privilege of using their property. . . . Even if we'd wanted to, we couldn't have paid. Adrian had watched to see where Miz Kelly kept the cash box. 'Twasn't only poker winnings he and Parker got away with!"

Tommy's hands clenched. "He stole from *her*—after all she did for him!"

"Well, I doubt he'll keep it long. She reported it to the police, but, better than that, the word's being passed amongst the fliers. There ain't many of them hasn't at least heard of Miz Kelly and her square dealing. I expect that Canuck's going to have a hard time stayin' outa sight."

George glanced up at his hostess. "This is a mighty good sandwich, ma'am. Sure do thank you." Ma blushed and nodded.

"But what about the show closing?" Mark asked. "What happened to everyone?"

"Well, Miz Kelly made a speech about feeling real bad about having to let us go. I expect, though, she was kinda glad to be through with the responsibility. That last squeak-out Jeff pulled just about did her in.

"Anyway, Yank and Noah said they'd been hearing a lot about this new Air Mail Service and how they was hiring pilots. They decided to head East and see if they could get taken on. Miz Kelly sold her two planes and bought one of them racing jobs. She planned to head for the races in Nebraska, where they're offering some fair prize money. Of course, you know Zeb and Teddy—where she goes, they go. So they're out there working as crew for her."

George paused, his eyes staring down at his big finger as it traced over and over the checked pattern in the tablecloth.

"And Jeff?" Tommy questioned.

"Yeah . . . Jeff." George sighed. "Somehow that miracle he pulled off in our last show made him think he could get away with any stunt in the world—and with paying passengers. I argued that if he was going to try that, we'd have to spend a lot of time and money to give our Jenny a good going-over first. He just wouldn't see it—called me a 'scared old maid.'

"So we broke up the partnership. He give me his share from the show that day and an IOU for the rest of our Jenny. And Miz Kelly sold me her Jenny for my little bit of savings and another IOU."

"So Jeff is barnstorming all on his own now," Tommy concluded.

"No, Tom, Jeff is dead." George's voice broke slightly on the last word. Tommy could sense his effort as he went on, his voice holding to an expressionless monotone. It was as if the only way George could tell the story was to say the words without letting his mind linger on their meaning.

"I heard that Jeff went up pretty high to start a loop —at least he'd learned never to make the mistake of starting too low again. They say when he went into his dive for speed, he just got going faster than that old Jenny was ever built to take. I don't even know if he realized it—you know how much we could trust those instruments. When he started to pull out, one of the wings just tore off and fluttered down like a leaf off a tree."

George swallowed hard, raised his head and gave a sad smile. "The only good thing about it was—his passenger lived. God alone knows why. Somehow the fellow was thrown clear and landed in a swampy area that cushioned his fall."

He jumped to his feet. "So that's the tally. And Teddy said you had a place here big enough to land on, so I thought I'd come up and land on it. But I didn't know you were making a regular thing of it. How about showing me your setup?"

The men rose quickly and headed for the outdoors, eager to be away from the sadness that hung above the kitchen table. Ma brushed away quick tears for a foolish man she had never known and began to clear the dishes.

Tommy found it hard to speak. He was glad when Mark took the lead in showing George the facilities that had been set up for the mail planes. George, too, was very quiet, at first, but he seemed glad for the distraction. After a while he began to ask interested questions.

At the end of the tour George made a sudden gesture toward the road. "What's so interesting over there?"

Surprised, Tommy, Pap, and Mark looked where he was pointing. A majority of the spectators who had come to see the mail plane were still there. "It's your plane," Tommy explained. "People around here just can't seem to get enough of watching airplanes. They're hoping you'll be taking off soon."

"Is that a fact?" George replied slowly. "Well, that sure is encouraging for an idea that's been ticklin' my mind. Let's set down here a minute and do some figgering." Without seeming to help him, George pushed a wooden box forward for Pap to sit on, then he and Tommy and Mark sat cross-legged on the grass.

"You know, I've been finding a lot of little towns like this," George began. "People in them haven't been bored by airplanes yet—like those in the bigger places that the air shows played. Folks in these back areas are eager for rides. Not only that, there's quite a few people want to learn to fly. I've been thinking that a fellow with an airplane and a nice strip of land might do right well setting up his own little airport and flying school. . . . Well, what do you think? I got the airplane . . ."

"And we got the strip of land, huh?" Pap interrupted. "But there's one big difference. Our land's paid for— your plane ain't. Even without debt, it sounds to me like a pretty shaky business."

"It's not much of a debt, Mr. Davison," George was quick to answer. "I've already paid off more 'n half what I owe Miz Kelly. By sticking to the small backwater towns, I've been earning right good money this summer."

"This *summer*," Pap mocked. "But soon it'll be fall, and then cold weather. Won't be many people wanting to fly then."

"I think you'll be surprised. My guess is that only snowstorms and tornadoes will keep them away. But if worse comes to worst, we could always take the ship south during the really bad weather."

Tommy's heart was racing, and while George defended his plan, Tommy searched his mind for the argument that would convince Pap. Suddenly he thought he had it. "Listen, Pap, aren't you always saying that any good farmer gets as much use as possible out of his land?"

Pap eyed him with suspicion. "So?"

"Well, look, here's the north field already being used as an air strip, so we can't farm it. But the mail's coming through only two, three times a week. The field's just— lying fallow the rest of the time." Tommy leaned closer to his father. "With what we could make selling rides and lessons, that field would be bringing in at least twice as much as now—and that cash money, too."

Tommy watched Pap's face. Reluctant to admit quickened interest, his father had not quite been able to hide the effect of those last words.

"Well, I'll be durned!" Mark said. "Sounds like we've found us a new cash crop—airplanes!"

"Hold on now, boys," Pap growled. "I never said yes. We'd have to do a lot of thinkin' on how to set this up."

George, his face thoughtful, was eying Pap's two casts. "One thing sure," he said. "We'd need someone with experience to help us set up our bookkeeping. It takes know-how to run a business."

Pap glared at him. "You think running a farm is a picnic? I'll bet I've kept books for a lot more years than you been flyin' airplanes." He held out his right arm. "Just let me get this one cast off next week, and I can show you anything you need to know in that line."

"Why, that'd be wonderful, Mr. Davison!" George continued to press his advantage. "I guess there ain't much farmin' can be done one-handed, but we sure could use your head on the figgerin' and paperwork. . . . Might even be a bit of a change for you, while you're still mending."

"Might at that," Pap admitted.

Tommy watched the gleam enter his father's eyes at the thought of getting back to some kind of satisfying work.

"Hurray!" Mark exploded. "*Letic and Davison Flying School* now opening at Anna's Corner Airport."

"Just a minute there." Pap glared at Mark, then at George. "If Tommy's going to pay off the other half of that airplane of yours, and I'm providing the land, I think we ought to call it *Davison and Letic*." He struggled to his feet before the new partners could recover from their surprise. "Well, c'mon, boys. Don't get so carried away you forget you've got work to be done."

Head high, Pap stalked away toward the house. Mark jumped up and made for the barn. But George and Tommy just sat on for a while, grinning foolishly at each other.

Chapter

19

TOMMY WATCHED SOME LEAVES DRIFTING DOWN AND sniffed at the still-new smell of their little building before he opened the door of the office. He was startled to find his partner bent over the desk, his hands clutching at an area below his ribs.

"What is it?" Tommy asked. "Are you in pain?"

George tried to straighten. "Uh . . . no . . ." he grunted. "It's really nothing, Tom. Touch of indigestion. Guess I've been overdoing it on your ma's good cooking."

With concern Tommy noted the way George was breathing—short gasping pants. Though the day was not warm, perspiration had formed all around George's hairline. "You look awful!" Tommy said. "Better get into town and let Doc McNally check you over."

"On a beautiful Sunday like this—dead calm and not a

cloud in the sky?" George was struggling to breathe normally. "With a mail plane due in? C'mon, Tom, you know we need the both of us to handle things today." He forced a smile and stood up straight. "Look, the pain's leaving already. It's just like I said—a little heartburn. But I'll make you a promise—if it happens again, I'll run in and see Doc. In fact, the way he's got the flying bug, I may be able to swap an examination for a free flying lesson!"

In spite of his worry, Tommy had to smile. Dr. McNally was only one of the many local residents who spent all their spare moments watching the mail planes, paying to take an occasional ride, and observing the wobbly practice flights of student pilots. Some people, Tommy had heard, were even talking of improving bumpy Oak Hill Road—now that it lead to the town's first airport.

Whatever had caused George's pain, it seemed to be over. He began to chat in his usual gossipy fashion. "That plane from New York's past due. Should have been right on time with weather like this." George glanced out the window, then gave a low whistle. "Well, well. Will you look at the dandy who's come to join the common folks!"

Tommy turned around. "Say, that's no ordinary dandy. That's C. G. Smith, boss of our air mail service. Hope he's not here to complain."

"Nah, he's out for a Sunday drive. Look, he's got his wife and kid with him. Nice lookin' woman, though I think I'd object if my wife wore a dress that short," George mused.

Tommy went out to greet the Smiths and discovered

George was right. Mr. Smith explained that he and his wife—it was immediately obvious that he would never object to anything she did—had driven out to watch the mail plane arrive and depart.

"And to get me a ride, Daddy. Don't forget—you promised!" insisted his small daughter.

"I said we'd see, darling," Mr. Smith temporized. "I really doubt that you'd like flying." Tommy tried not to grin, remembering how Mr. Smith, himself, loathed the flights he had to make.

"I'm seven years old today, and you said I could have a ride if I wanted, and I *do*," the persistent young lady repeated.

Tommy knelt down to be at eye level with the child. "No one can take a ride just now, sweetheart," he explained. "First the mail plane has to arrive and be taken care of. Then we'll start selling rides." He looked up. "Listen! There it is now!"

All eyes were turned to the east as the roar of the engine grew louder. Soon the plane, a Standard, came into view. The pleasure of the watchers was evident. Parents stooped to lift offspring to their shoulders so that the children could see over the crowd.

But all Tommy's attention was on the sound the engine was making—a popping, struggling noise that might mean real trouble. He murmured, "Good for you!" when the mail pilot made a straight-in approach and shut the engine down as soon as he was on the ground. Maybe the motor hadn't been ruined if a man of experience had been nursing it along.

The pilot jumped to the ground and pulled off his helmet to reveal a thatch of sandy white hair. "Noah!"

Tommy and George said together. The partners glanced at each other. George, as always, was generous. "You go ahead, Tom. You need to look at that plane—I can talk with him later." He turned back to those who were waiting to purchase rides in the Jenny.

"Well, Tommy!" Noah beamed. "My luck's still holding!"

The two pumped hands, then Tommy jerked a thumb at Noah's plane. "What happened?"

"What usually happens when you get into a freezing rain?"

"Ice?"

"Ice—on the wings *and* the prop." Settling into his story, Noah leaned against the fuselage. "Halfway across those miserable mountains, I ran into a granddaddy of a wind. Blew me way off course. Next thing I was in a fog you coulda carved statues from. Before long I didn't have an idea where the passes were."

He ran a hand through his hair. "Well, fellas who've lived to tell about flying this route had told me, 'If you're lost and got poor visibility, get up *high*—enough to clear the tallest peak.' So I climbed. But then I was in that rain, and I saw the ice start building. When it got on the prop, the thing started vibrating until I thought it would shake my teeth loose. No engine's gonna take *that* for long."

While he listened, Tommy climbed onto a wing and stretched forward, trying to see how much damage the engine had taken. Noah continued. "I started going higher, looking for warmer air, but just then the engine started making that infernal racket and lost power. 'Course the only way to go then was down! I finally did find some air warm enough to melt the ice off. But that engine kept right on spitting and sputtering."

Tommy shook his head. "No chance of climbing back to a safe altitude with it acting like that!"

Noah nodded. "No chance! I tell you, Tom, I never did so much praying in my life—begging that that fog would blow away before I flew myself into the side of a mountain. And, glory be, all of a sudden, I flew out into this beautiful blue sky!"

"But how'd you find us?"

"It wasn't easy! I dropped to darn near treetop level, trying to figure out where I was, but I didn't recognize a thing. And then—so help me, Tom, there's a farmer southeast of here that I'm planning to kiss!"

Tommy laughed. "I'd like to see you try it! What did he do?"

"Bless him for an air-minded saint! He's painted on his barn roof, in big black letters, *Anna's Corner Airport* —with an arrow pointing this way. If I hadn't seen that, by now I'd be sitting in some God-forsaken pasture—if I was lucky."

Finishing his quick inspection of the engine, Tommy smiled. "Noah, you'll be happy to know I don't think that noise was a blown cylinder. Instead of a new motor, we're going to get away with putting in a new spark plug! Let's go get some help to push it out of the way so George can start flying."

"George!" Noah's eyebrows lifted as he spotted the sign on the new building. *"Davison and Letic, Flight School and Pleasure Rides,"* he read aloud. "You and old George *teaching* flying? Why, you'd hardly learned how yourself!"

"Sh-h-h!" Tommy cautioned, grinning. "Want to destroy my students' confidence?"

"Seriously, Tom, how's it working out?"

"Not bad—better than we figured, in fact. Of course, the mail contract helps, but you'd be amazed how many folks around here want to learn to fly. We're nearly breaking even—without the contract."

With many willing helpers, the Standard was soon pushed in from the runway. After a few minutes of catching up on old times, George sighed. "Have to go on with this later, Noah." He walked out to where his passengers stood waiting.

While Tommy worked on the Standard, he was amused to observe that Mr. Smith was under siege. As each satisfied rider alighted from his short trip, Tommy heard the small daughter pleading harder. When the pretty mother added a word, her husband surrendered. He came up to Tommy, opening his wallet.

No one else wanted a ticket and the repair job was done, so Tommy and Noah took a moment to watch George land. Tommy was surprised as the plane bounced down hard. That might be a normal landing for some pilots, but for George it was sloppy.

George was obviously relieved when he realized that the Smith child was the last passenger waiting. Tommy almost stepped forward with an offer to fly this trip. Then he stopped, remembering that his first duty lay in getting the Standard gassed and Noah on his way.

"I wanna fly in the back seat," the seven-year-old was saying. "You can't see as well if you sit in front." The child pointed to the upper wings, which did somewhat obstruct the view from the front seat.

George, obliging as ever, climbed out of the rear seat and helped her into it.

"Just circle the field a few times, Letic," Smith requested in high, nervous tones. "Don't go out of sight." George nodded. Soon the Jenny lifted from the ground, its rear seat boasting a small hand energetically waving a pale blue handerchief.

Still talking, Tommy and Noah walked back and began to fill the Standard's gas tank. As they were finishing the job, Noah remarked, "Yank's starting on this route, too. You'll probably see him along here any day now."

"You two still sticking together, are you?" Tommy asked.

"Yeah, even boarding together. But we got to find better quarters. Last night I saw a cockroach under my bed so big . . ." Noah broke off. "What's the matter, Tom? What'd you see?"

Tommy had been facing the airplane watchers. "Something's wrong—come on!" He darted into the office to grab a pair of binoculars from the desk and ran out to where he could get a clear view of the Jenny.

The aircraft was still making a large circle above the field, but there was a roughness in the way she flew, more like the over-controlling of a student pilot than like George's usual smooth handling. The faces of the experienced spectators were worried as they sensed the difference, too. The Smiths, seeing Tommy focusing his field glasses, hurried toward him.

"Oh, no," Tommy whispered. "He's having another of those attacks!"

NOAH HAD SEIZED THE GLASSES. "LORDY, TOM, HE'S HOLD-ing onto his stomach as if it was full of hot coals! He'll never be able to land that thing, the shape he's in!"

Tommy glimpsed a familiar face among the spectators. Brushing past the Smiths, he ran to Doc. Without pream-ble, he described the pain George had experienced that morning. "Will this go away, too, Doc? Will he be able to get down okay?"

Doc lowered his own binoculars and glared at Tommy. "I don't diagnose by long distance, young man. How-ever, *if* I played guessing games, I'd say that either his heart or his appendix is bad. He might be lucky and have the attack subside. On the other hand, he's just as likely to pass out."

"Adele, my baby!" Mrs. Smith screamed, sinking

into a startled Noah's arms. He passed her swiftly to her white-faced husband.

Biting hard on his lower lip, Noah muttered, "Tom, I've got a crazy idea. He looked from Tom to the Standard. Tommy understood at once. He nodded, and Noah eyed Mr. Smith. "Of course, it's against regulations."

"Regulations be damned!" Mr. Smith exploded. "If there's anything you can do to get my little girl down safely, do it!"

"Come on, Tom!" Noah raced for the mail plane.

Tommy detoured to grab up a large roll of heavy rope. "We just bought this for the hay hoist in the barn. If you're thinking what I'm thinking, we're going to need it."

Together the two fliers tied the rope securely to the Standard's undercarriage, making a few knots in its length while they cast frequent glances upward. The Jenny was still making its circle, but it was obvious that George was fighting hard to maintain control. Quickly Tommy secured the heavy coils of rope to the axle bar with a piece of baling wire, while Noah climbed into the cockpit. Tom hurried to the front of the Standard, breathing a silent prayer as he called out, "Switch on?"

"Switch on!" returned Noah, and Tommy pulled the huge propeller through with all of his strength. As if it had never given a moment's trouble, the engine produced a reliable-sounding roar. Tommy ran around to the wing, climbed up past Noah, and dropped into the mail compartment. He sat high, balancing as best he could on a bulky sack. Noah was already taxiing out when Tommy gave him the go signal.

It seemed to take ages to climb to where the Jenny continued her wallowing circle. Glancing down, Tommy saw Ma, Pap, and Mark joining the crowd below. "Well," he thought, "I'm afraid they're about to find out that those stunts weren't quite as easy as I made them sound."

As Noah leveled out at the proper altitude above the Jenny and matched its speed, he leaned forward, a worried crease in his forehead. "You know I never actually did this stunt before, Tom," he yelled.

"Well, you better have been watching darn close, then," Tommy yelled back. He was pulling off his heavy farm shoes. "Just concentrate on keeping that Jenny's prop as far away from me and the rope as you can. Stay back, but not so far back that I can't reach the cockpit." He attempted a feeble joke. "I *could* land on the tail and crawl forward, but I don't want to show off."

For once in his life Noah looked completely serious. "Good luck, Tom."

"Good luck to all of us," Tommy muttered as he climbed out onto the wing and worked his way down onto the axle bar, "and lots of it!"

The wind was whipping Tommy's hair into his eyes as he struggled to release the baling wire. In the past he'd thought of his white circus helmet merely as part of a flamboyant costume. Now he realized how much it had helped to keep down both his hair and the terrible, whistling wind noise. The coveralls, too, had been a good idea he discovered when his shirt tail was tugged from inside his trousers and began to flap wildly.

The rope fell free. "No time to wish I'd dressed for the occasion," Tommy thought. "Here goes!" He gave one quick test tug on the rope and then was swinging down, hand over hand, as quickly as he could go.

When Tommy looked down, George was staring up at him. He seemed to be holding the Jenny more steady— fighting hard to match the speed and direction of the Standard above.

Tommy was very close now; he could see the fright in the little girl's wide eyes as she watched his descent. Yet she had not panicked. She could help, if she would. "What did her mother call her?" Tommy pondered. "Della? No, that's not it, but, oh heck, it's close enough."

"Della, Dell, honey. Listen," Tommy shouted. "I'm coming down to get in with you. Give me some room."

She nodded and at once slid forward and sidewise, squeezing herself into the smallest possible space. The rope blew back, carrying him too far behind the Jenny. Perhaps he had made a mistake warning Noah not to get near the prop. No, Noah was correcting now, edging forward.

Tommy's heart lurched as his sweaty hands began to slide, but they were stopped almost at once by one of the knots. He felt into space with his feet. The cockpit should be there. He should be touching it now. As he craned his neck, trying to see, he felt two little hands, not pulling, but gently guiding his feet to touch each side of the cockpit. He thanked Adele by falling heavily on top of her.

"Are you hurt?" he shouted, trying to move out of her way.

The little person lay still for a moment, then took a deep breath. "No, but I don't want to play this anymore. I want to go *down*."

Tommy laughed. "I don't want to play anymore either, honey," he answered in relief. He leaned forward to yell, "Lie back and relax, George. I've got it!" His partner slumped backward, as Tommy's hands closed over the stick.

Doc had organized things on the ground. From the time the Standard touched down, not a minute was wasted. After a cursory inspection, the physician announced that George's appendix was probably the culprit. "I don't think it's burst yet—that's a blessing. Here, Pete. Let's get him to Middleton fast!"

The most comfortable car available had already been commandeered. Its owner and Doc, with a lot of willing help, bundled George into it and sped away. Tommy and Noah sank into camp chairs shoved forward by several bystanders. Noah sighed. "You know, Tom, I don't believe I'd care to do that for a living."

"I certainly agree with you, Noah. Absolutely. That's far too dangerous for a businessman like me."

Tommy looked up to see Mr. and Mrs. Smith standing before them. Unaware or uncaring that there were tears in their eyes, each parent held tightly to one of Adele's hands.

"I always thought all fliers—and especially barnstormers—were idiots," Smith began, looking at Noah. "I'd like to apologize for that." He held out a trembling hand. "I want you to know I'm planning to recommend a large raise in your salary."

Noah shook the hand, muttering an embarrassed, "Glad we could help."

In turn, Smith offered his hand to Tommy. "And if

that 'businessman' ever decides he'd like a job flying the mail, he's got it. Just get in touch with my office."

"Well, thank you, Mr. Smith." Tommy glanced across at Pap. "When the day comes that *Davison and Letic* can manage without me, I might want to take you up on that. It'll be a while, I guess, with both my partners having to mend first. But when you get those better planes and don't need our refueling stop, there might be just enough business here for the two of them."

"I betcha we'll be flying clear across the whole country by then," piped Adele's clear voice.

Tommy leaned forward, placing both hands on her shoulders. "Now, *you've* convinced me! Always did itch to see San Francisco. I'll be there, Mr. Smith."

"Hogwash!" said Pap. "There'll never be a plane that can cross the Rocky Mountains. You're talking nonsense again, Tom!"

Tommy studied his father. Under the bluster in Pap's voice, he detected a note of pride—and almost a dare.

"You'll see the day, Pap," Tommy answered with confidence. "You'll see the day we fly the Rockies. And I hope I'm the first!" He laughed over his father's protest. "And when you think I'm not around, you'll be betting everyone that I can do it!"

Bibliography

Bach, Richard. *Nothing by Chance*. New York: William Morrow and Co., 1969.

Bruno, Harry. *Wings over America: The Story of American Aviation*. Garden City, N.Y.: Halcyon House, 1944.

Buchanan, Lamont. *The Flying Years*. New York: G. P. Putnam's Sons, 1953.

Caidin, Martin. *Barnstorming: The Great Years of Stunt Flying*. New York: Duell, Sloan, and Pearce, 1965.

Dwiggins, Don. *The Air Devils*. Philadelphia and New York: J. B. Lippincott Co., 1966.

———. *The Barnstormers: Flying Daredevils of the Roaring Twenties*. New York: Grosset and Dunlap, 1968.

Funderburk, Thomas R. *The Early Birds of War: The Daring Pilots and Fighter Airplanes of World War I*. New York: Grosset and Dunlap, 1968.

Glines, Carroll V. *The Saga of the Air Mail*. Princeton, N.J.: D. Van Nostrand Co., 1968.

Gurney, Gene. *Flying Aces of World War I*. New York: Random House, 1965.

Josephy, Alvin M., ed. *The American Heritage of Flight*. New York: American Heritage Publishing Co., 1962.

Kelly, Charles J., Jr. *The Sky's the Limit*. New York: Coward-McCann, 1963.

Lincke, Jack R. *Jenny Was No Lady: The Story of the JN-4D*. New York: W. W. Norton and Co., 1970

Lindbergh, Charles A. *"We"*. New York: G. P. Putnam's Sons, 1927.

Nielson, Dale, ed. *Saga of the U.S. Air Mail Service, 1918–1927*. Miami, Florida: 1962.

Rogers, Agnes, and Allen, Frederick Lewis. *I Remember Distinctly: A Family Album of the American People, 1918–1941*. New York: Harper and Brothers, 1947.

Roseberry, C. R., *The Challenging Skies*. New York: Doubleday and Co., 1966.

Rowe, Captain Basil L. *Under My Wings*. Indianapolis and New York: The Bobbs-Merrill Co., 1956.

Shamburger, Page. *Tracks Across the Sky*. Philadelphia and New York: J. B. Lippincott Co., 1964.

Smith, Dean C. *By the Seat of My Pants*. Boston: Little, Brown, and Co., 1961.

Stilwell, Hart, and Rodgers, Slats. *Old Soggy No. 1: The Uninhibited Story of Slats Rodgers*. New York: Julian Messner, 1954.

Sunderman, Major James F., USAF, ed. *Early Air Pioneers. 1862–1935*. New York: Franklin Watts, 1961.

Tallman, Frank. *Flying the Old Airplanes*. Garden City, New York: Doubleday and Co., 1973.

Taylor, Frank. *High Horizons*. New York: McGraw-Hill Book Co., 1962.

This Fabulous Century, vol. 2, *1919–1920*. New York: Time-Life Books, 1969.

Webb, Foster A. *War Maneuvers and Stunt Flying*. Flint, Michigan: Universal Supply Co., 1940.

Whitehouse, Arthur. *The Sky's the Limit*. New York: The Macmillan Co., 1971.

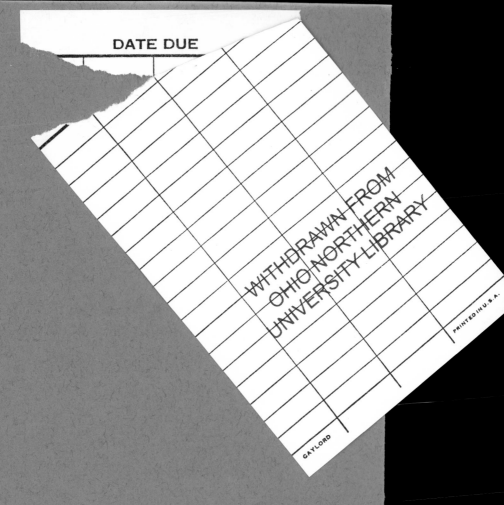